Gwen STEFANI

Biography

Gwen STEFANI

KGL

Katherine Krohn

Twenty-First Century Books
Minneapolis

*For Markie and Lucy Jo, two **great** kids*

Twenty-First Century Books
A division of Lerner Publishing Group, Inc.
241 First Avenue North
Minneapolis, MN 55401 U.S.A.

Website addresses: www.lernerbooks.com
                   www.biography.com

Library of Congress Cataloging-in-Publication Data

Krohn, Katherine E.
    Gwen Stefani / by Katherine Krohn.
       p.   cm. — (Biography)
    Includes bibliographical references (p.   ) and index.
    ISBN 978–0–8225–7157–5 (lib. bdg. : alk. paper)
    1. Stefani, Gwen, 1969– —Juvenile literature. 2. Singers—United
States—Biography—Juvenile literature. I. Title.
    ML3930.S74K76 2008
    782.42164092—dc22 [B]   2007000120

Manufactured in the United States of America
1 2 3 4 5 6 – JR – 13 12 11 10 09 08

CONTENTS

Linda Perry (right) *challenged Gwen* (left) *to express herself in solo performance as well as with her band, No Doubt.*

INTRODUCTION

Gwen Stefani was terrified. Her heart pounded, and her brown eyes welled with tears. For seventeen years, Gwen had worked and performed with her award-winning band, No Doubt. Though Gwen felt scared, she knew she was ready to leave the nest. She was ready to make her first solo album.

Gwen, 33, was still exhausted from No Doubt's 2002 *Rock Steady* concert tour. She had hoped to ease into the new project slowly. But Jimmy Iovine—Gwen's boss at Interscope Records, her record label—had other ideas. He wanted to pair Stefani with a top-notch songwriter. He chose Linda Perry, lead singer of the band 4 Non Blondes. Perry had written hits for pop stars such as Christina Aguilera and Pink. And Perry's time was precious.

Stefani remembered, "The record company called me and was like, 'You've got to go work with Linda Perry. Now. She only has five days out of the whole year to work with you.' And I'd just got off tour!" Stefani felt burned out. She had barely had a chance to see her husband, whom she had just recently married.

But Stefani knew she had no choice but to get back to work. She could vacation another time, she figured. And she felt excited about the new project. She planned to make a fun dance record that featured the kind of music she loved in the 1980s.

At first Stefani felt awkward trying to write songs with Linda Perry. Stefani was used to writing songs with her friends, the guys in No Doubt. The first day Stefani and Perry met, they wrote a song together called "Fine by You." Stefani felt satisfied with her first attempt to write with a stranger. "I went home and felt good, like, 'I did it. I wrote a song today.'" But she was still nervous about going back.

By the time Stefani and Perry met again the next day, Perry had composed another song. It was called "What You Waiting For?" and was a message for Stefani to find her confidence with her writing and express herself. Stefani felt jealous that Perry had written a song so quickly. She also felt pushed a bit.

"It was like a dare, and I don't even remember writing the words after that," said Stefani. "I just barfed them out."

Gwen's solo album *Love.Angel.Music.Baby.* was released in November 2004. It was quick to make a splash on the *Billboard* music charts and in MTV video ratings. The album generated five hit singles and videos. "Hollaback Girl" was the record's biggest hit. It was the first song by any U.S. recording artist to sell one million legal downloads. The album propelled the singer into solo stardom.

After the release of *Love.Angel.Music.Baby.*, Stefani kept busy. She followed up her first solo success with a second, 2006's *The Sweet Escape*. She made her silver-screen debut in the film *The Aviator*, playing a glamorous old-Hollywood star on the arm of Howard Hughes, played by Leonardo DiCaprio. Already a style icon known for her unpredictable, edgy fashion sense, she has become one of the hottest new designers of clothing and accessories. And she shows no signs of slowing down.

Gwen Stefani has shown the world she is a versatile performer and multitalented celebrity. "She's got an extraordinary mixture of the elements that make a great pop star and the elements that make a great rock star," says Gwen's friend Shirley Manson, of the band Garbage. "She seems very benign and wholesome, but underneath lurks an incredible toughness and powerful directness. Nobody can copy her, because she's this uniquely extraordinary contradiction."

Gwen grew up in Anaheim, California.

Chapter **ONE**

ORANGE COUNTY GIRL

ON OCTOBER 3, 1969, GWEN RENEE STEFANI was born in Fullerton, California. Gwen's father, Dennis, worked as a marketing executive for Yamaha motorcycles. Patti, Gwen's mother, worked as a dental assistant.

Baby Gwen was the second of four children, two years younger than her brother Eric. In 1972 her sister, Jill, was born. Her younger brother, Todd, was born in 1974.

Gwen's family lived near Fullerton in Anaheim, Orange County, a suburb of Los Angeles. Anaheim is the home of both Disneyland and the Anaheim Angels baseball team. Millions of tourists each year flock to the city to enjoy its warm weather, the nearby Pacific Ocean, and the many theme parks and attractions in the area.

1969: AN EVENTFUL YEAR

The year of Gwen's birth included several milestones for U.S. culture. Among them:

- In March, the Levi Strauss Company introduced their first bell-bottomed jeans.
- On July 20, American astronauts Neil Armstrong and Edwin "Buzz" Aldrin of *Apollo 11* became the first men to land on the moon. TV viewers from around the world watched in awe as Armstrong took his legendary first step on the moon's surface.
- Pilot episodes of *The Brady Bunch* and *Sesame Street* aired on U.S. television in the fall.

AN EXCITING TIME

Gwen was born during a dynamic time in the United States. Richard Milhous Nixon was president, and the U.S. military was fighting in the Vietnam War (1954–1975). A growing counterculture movement was spreading across the country. A counterculture is made up of people who oppose social or political norms. One of the defining characteristics of the young countercul-ture was its strong stance against the war. Throughout 1969 anti-war demonstrators protested the U.S. involve-ment in Vietnam. One month after Gwen was born, a quarter of a million people held a peace demonstration outside the White House in Washington, D.C. Earlier in the year, newlyweds John Lennon and Yoko Ono had held a "bed-in" for peace. Covered only in sheets, the happy couple answered questions from the press while lying in bed. They discussed their hope for peace and an end to the war.

The counterculture also defined itself largely through its music. The music industry was buzzing with talented and innovative performers. Hit songs by the British rock band the Rolling Stones and the American folk band Peter, Paul, and Mary soared to the top of the music charts. In August the legendary Woodstock Music and Art Festival, known simply as Woodstock, took place in northern New York State. It featured musicians such as The Grateful Dead, Joan Baez, Jimi Hendrix, and Janis Joplin. Four hundred thousand young people attended the three-day rock concert. The concert would be remembered as a landmark counterculture, or "hippie," event.

As a child of the years that followed, Gwen was free-spirited and happy. Her parents taught her to appreciate music from an early age. Dennis and Patti Stefani were in a little-known folk band called The Innertubes. Gwen's dad played the guitar, and her mom played the harp. Albums by Bob Dylan and Emmylou Harris spun on her parents' record player. Gwen's mom and dad also took their children to live musical performances. One of the first concerts Gwen ever saw was an Emmylou Harris concert. It was at the Palomino Club, a well-known Los Angeles performance spot at the time.

A Girl Called "Sunshine"

Growing up, Gwen loved to pretend, and she enjoyed playing dress-up. Her mom was a talented seamstress and made the children elaborate Halloween costumes. Gwen's mom also taught her to sew. Gwen was a creative child, and she enjoyed the process of turning fabric into something beautiful, stylish, or fun to wear.

Gwen and her brother Eric sometimes made up funny puppet shows and performed for friends and neighbors. Eric played the piano and wrote songs. Gwen sang along. Gwen also made up a game called Musical House with her sister, Jill. Instead of talking to each other, they'd sing everything.

Gwen liked school too. But schoolwork wasn't always easy for her. She had trouble with spelling. "It was really challenging for me," she admitted. "I still can't spell that well." Gwen has dyslexia, a learning disability that changes the way the brain processes written material. People with dyslexia usually have challenges with reading, writing, and spelling. Dyslexia has nothing to do with intelligence—dyslexics are often bright and creative.

When Gwen was young, she also had issues with her weight. "I think I went on my first diet in sixth grade," Stefani said years later. "It's in my genes to be a little bigger and I don't like that, admittedly."

As a teenager, Gwen landed her first job, scrubbing floors at a Dairy Queen restaurant. Later she worked as a salesgirl at The Broadway, a department store in Los Angeles.

Jean Harlow (right) *is one of Gwen's favorite old-Hollywood stars. Harlow was one of the most popular actresses of the 1930s.*

Gwen had a wide variety of tastes and interests. She liked to watch TV reruns of black-and-white movies from the 1930s and 1940s. Gwen covered her bedroom walls with posters of Hollywood legends. She admired the way the early movie stars looked and acted. She loved the glamorous, elegant gowns and sparkly jewelry.

Gwen was also interested in Japanese trends. Her father often traveled to Japan on business trips for his job with Yamaha motorcycles. He would bring back souvenirs for Gwen. "I loved Hello Kitty and all these different Japanese things," Gwen remembered.

Gwen loved animals. In high school she got a pet dog, a blond, long-haired Lhasa apso named Maggen. She eventually nicknamed the dog "Lamb" because it followed Gwen everywhere, just as in the children's song "Mary Had a Little Lamb."

At Loara High School in Anaheim, Gwen made friends easily. She had a bubbly personality and lots of energy. Her nickname was "Sunshine." Naturally athletic, Gwen was on the school swim team. Because she was a good swimmer, her other nickname was "Frog." Gwen honed her musical talent at school too. She played the piccolo in the school marching band.

Gwen also had a good singing voice. She liked show tunes from musicals like *Annie* and *Evita*. But *The Sound of Music* was her favorite. Her first experience onstage was performing the hit song "On My Radio" in a high school talent show. Gwen's mom made her a special costume for the performance. It was a tweed dress just like one that Julie Andrews wore in the *The Sound of Music*.

AN EYE FOR DESIGN

Gwen and her friends had a creative hobby. They liked to go to local thrift stores and search the racks of used clothing. They would then take their purchases home and resew them. Gwen found that she had a special talent for making something original and interesting out of something old. She even liked to remake new clothes. "I'd go to . . . places like Wet Seal and Contempo Casuals, and try to find something weird," she said. Then she would remake it at home.

Gwen's room became crowded with clothing and

scraps of cloth. She experimented with fabric, color, and style. Sharp pins from her sewing projects were scattered around the floor. Gwen's family learned to always wear shoes when they visited her room.

Gwen liked to experiment with makeup too. She especially liked to imitate Hollywood glamour. Her trademark skinny eyebrows, dark mascara, and bold red lips are part of the early Hollywood look she started wearing as a teenager.

As she experimented with her look, Gwen developed her own unique style. She had an unusual way of putting clothing and accessories together. For example, she wore monkey boots (shorter combat boots) and tank tops with men's pajama bottoms she had pegged (tapered at the cuff). "She was very quiet growing up—a late bloomer," remembered Gwen's dad. "But she always put clothes together in an interesting way."

The band Madness, which inspired No Doubt, formed in London in the 1970s. Like other ska bands, the group fused Jamaican rhythms and melodies with punk rock music.

Chapter **TWO**

NO DOUBT

GWEN'S SIBLINGS WERE CREATIVE TOO. SHE ESPE-
cially admired her older brother, Eric. He was a cartoonist, played in his high school marching band, and
had "wild artist friends," according to Gwen. "I don't
know if he really was cool or not," she later reflected,
"but he seemed cool to me."

In December 1986, nineteen-year-old Eric decided to
form a band with his friend John Spence. Eric and
John really liked ska, a form of Jamaican music.
Gwen credits Eric with introducing her to ska. Eric
first brought home a record by Madness, a British ska
band. He played it constantly, and Gwen caught on to
the new sound too. Soon they were all entranced by
the unique musical style.

ROSKO

Desmond Dekker (at mike) *was one of the most popular ska and reggae musicians in Jamaica. His band was called The Aces.*

SKA'S THE LIMIT

The sound that influenced Eric, John, and Gwen in the 1980s was new to the Orange County teenagers. However, it was actually based on a style of music that had emerged earlier in Jamaica. In the 1960s, musicians such as Bob Marley and Desmond Dekker combined rhythm and blues, swing, early rock, and American jazz music with Caribbean mento and calypso. The result was a new musical genre (style) that soon became known as ska. Ska music is characterized by a medium tempo with beats two and four emphasized. It has a walking bass (a bass line that moves in steps with an even rhythm) and repeated rhythms on guitar or piano. Often horns fill out the piano's accompaniment.

The new sound attracted a following of stylish, hip fans. People in this ska subculture (smaller, distinct group within a larger culture) became known as "rude boys," taken from the Jamaican slang word for "hip" or "cool." Other musical styles such as rocksteady and reggae grew out of the new ska sound.

Ska music had a revival in the late 1970s in the United Kingdom. British ska bands like Madness, Bad Manners, and The Selecter took the original Jamaican sound and gave it a faster pace and hard-edged guitar chords. Their lyrics had a strong social or political message. The new generation of ska was called "Two Tone," after the British record company that produced many of the revival's hits. The name came from the two-tone (black-and-white) suits worn by the rude boys, as well as from the multiracial bands signed to the label.

Punk rock music was also popular in the 1970s in Britain, and Two Tone was tinged with the style and sensibility of that punk music. However, while ska was huge in Britain, no major United States recording companies had picked up the trend. As a result, there was no widespread, mainstream American interest in ska. But some people, mostly in large cities such as Los Angeles, San Francisco, New York, and Boston, took an interest in the revived genre. The new style generated a craze of ska fans and ska-playing musicians. These American "rude boys" and "rude girls" modeled themselves after the original rude boy subculture of Jamaica in the 1960s.

Eric and Gwen Stefani were growing up in Orange County as Two Tone was gathering a following there in the early 1980s. By the time Eric and John Spence had decided to form a band, they were hooked on the style. They wanted their band to play ska music too.

No Doubt Debuts

Eric was a talented musician—Gwen often woke up to his "banging" on the piano—but he couldn't sing. He asked Gwen to sing in the band. She would share lead vocals with John Spence. At the age of seventeen, Gwen didn't think of herself as a singer. She loved to sing just for fun. But it might be fun to sing in a band, she thought. Finally she told Eric yes.

At first, they called their three-person band Apple Corps. But they weren't sure if they really liked the name. One of John's favorite expressions was "no doubt." John got an idea—No Doubt would be a cooler name for a band, he figured. The new name stuck.

No Doubt gave their first official performance on March 12, 1987, at Fender's Ballroom in Long Beach, California. They performed second of fourteen bands, with the popular soul and ska band The Untouchables as the headline act.

That night, a high school junior named Tony Kanal was watching the performance. He thought No Doubt was great. A few weeks later, Tony tried out to be No Doubt's bass guitar player. The band members accepted him "even though [he'd] never been in a band, [had] long hair and [was] wearing Mexican sandals," they remembered.

No Doubt rehearsed in the Stefani family's garage. They practiced at least twice a week, after school or on the weekends. During the long hours of rehearsal, the band members became good friends. Gwen quickly developed a big crush on Tony Kanal. But she wasn't sure if Tony liked her. One night, as they were walking home from a party, Gwen asked Tony to kiss her. After that moment, Gwen still wasn't sure how Tony felt, but she knew she was in love. In time, the two began dating. Tony was organized and sure of himself—the opposite of Gwen. A natural leader, Tony acted as the band's manager. "Tony took care of everyone and he was on top of all the business," said Stefani.

When Gwen met Tony, she was really into ska music. Tony liked ska, but he liked popular dance music too, especially Prince. Because of Gwen's crush on Tony, she also became interested in artists like Prince, Lisa Lisa, and Debbie Deb.

Gwen listened to Prince's records and tried to sing like him. But it wasn't easy. She soon realized that his sound was unique—that no one but Prince could sound like Prince. Especially, she admitted, not "a white girl from Orange County."

Gwen also admired Sting, then a member of the band The Police. When she was sixteen, her dad took her to one of The Police's concerts. Gwen was thrilled when her dad (with help from a coworker) gave Gwen a backstage pass and the opportunity to meet Sting. With her father's encouragement, Gwen got up the nerve to talk to Sting. But the encounter was disappointing. Stefani later recalled her experience as an overweight, awkward teenager, shyly asking Sting for an autograph. "He was really mean. But I still loved him."

A TERRIBLE TRAGEDY

In December 1987, the band landed their first major gig. They were slated to play at the Roxy Theater in Hollywood. Band member John Spence pushed the band to rehearse hard to prepare for the gig. They practiced every day after school. No one in the band expected what was about to happen.

Tragically, on December 21, John committed suicide. Only eighteen years old, he was found dead in a parking lot in Anaheim. He had shot himself. John left behind a two-page suicide note saying good-bye to his family and friends.

"None of us were prepared for that, none of us could see that coming," said Tony Kanal. "It just changed everything."

The unexpected loss was also traumatic for Gwen. "I think it taught us all a big lesson in how much one person can influence so many different people," she said.

Gwen, Eric, and Tony were devastated. John was their good friend. Without him, No Doubt wouldn't have existed. After much soul-searching, the band decided to go ahead and perform at the Roxy engagement a few days later. That's what John would have wanted, they decided.

In 1989 No Doubt played for the Clean & Sober Beach Party in Newport, California. The lineup included Gwen (center), *Adrian Young* (left), *and Tony Kanal* (right).

GOING WITH THE FLOW

In the spring of 1988, the No Doubt roster changed once again. The band brought in a talented heavy-metal guitarist, a college music student named Tom Dumont. As they continued to perform, No Doubt soon had a loyal following of "rude boys" and "rude girls," fashioned after the Jamaican subculture that loved ska music.

A year later, Adrian Young joined the band. A skilled drummer, Adrian told the band that he had years of experience even though he had only one. Adrian was so talented that the band didn't care that he had lied about his experience. Gwen especially liked what Adrian brought to the band. "I'm gaudy and cheesy and I always want to push it. Adrian was always the yang of the band, if I was the yin," Gwen said in 2004. "I'm the cheese, he's the cool. That's what makes No Doubt."

Gwen enjoyed performing in the band. But she didn't really see herself as a serious musician. Her brother wrote the songs for the band. *He* was the songwriter, the committed, serious musician, she thought. Gwen just liked to be a part of the group. It was fun. She could hang out with her friends and spend lots of time with her boyfriend. "I was completely passive," she recalled. "I was in love with Tony and just happy to be in the band."

Gwen and Tony had fallen in love. After high school, Gwen figured she'd get married to Tony and have kids. She didn't dream about being an international pop star or successful musician. Gwen daydreamed about being a wife and mother.

Each day at school, Gwen did her best to learn, but her dyslexia made it difficult. When Gwen was growing up, people weren't as aware of learning disabilities such as dyslexia. Dyslexics can learn to read and process information more efficiently, but Gwen didn't have that kind of help in school.

Because Gwen had such a hard time concentrating on her lessons or listening to her teachers, she thought of herself as lazy. During school she escaped into daydreams. Sometimes she spent the whole class period sketching her boyfriend's name in artistic letters. "It was hard for me to learn," she recalled. "I couldn't even pay attention."

GLAM GIRL

Gwen was thrilled when Tony invited her to the prom. Gwen wanted a special dress for the event. She thought about how much she liked glamorous gowns, the kind that actresses wore in the old movies she liked to watch. Gwen remembered that she had admired the dress that actress Grace Kelly wore in the 1954 Alfred Hitchcock film *Rear Window*. She asked her mom to help her make one just like it. Gwen's mom made a beautiful black velvet and white chiffon gown, adorned with lots of sequins that Gwen sewed on herself. The dress reflected the elegant and dramatic style that Gwen had appreciated from an early age.

Tony's parents were Indian, and Gwen also admired the traditional Indian fashions that his mother wore.

In Rear Window, *Grace Kelly* (right) *played a fashion model. Her character's boyfriend, played by James Stewart, thinks he may have witnessed a murder.*

"She'd get all made up, with her sari and her jewels on, and I thought she was so glamorous," remembered Gwen. So Stefani adopted part of the cultural style into her own look. She started wearing a stick-on earring on her forehead as a bindi, a traditional forehead decoration worn by South Asian women.

Gwen enjoyed creating costumes for her No Doubt performances. She had a unique way of blending fashions to create her own style. She was soon copied by girls all over Orange County who loved ska music. Her favorite accessories included leather and chains, fishnet stockings, and wrist warmers. She liked to wear big, baggy, boys' pants from thrift stores or roomy men's pajama bottoms. Originally Gwen chose to wear big pants simply because she didn't like the looks of her lower half. With the loose-fitting pants, Gwen typically threw on a super-tight T-shirt or a tummy-exposing midriff top. Sometimes she'd wear clunky combat boots or monkey boots. To top off her look, Gwen liked to wear striking makeup: deep-red lipstick, heavy mascara, and eyeliner.

Although her outfits often included men's clothing, Gwen is a self-defined girly-girl. "But I definitely can hang out with the guys in the band because we have music in common," she has said. "They're like my brothers." She enjoys the dual aspects of her personality. She added, "I love that contradiction of being feminine but playing in the boys' treehouse. My whole life's been like that."

She Didn't See It

After high school, Gwen started taking art classes at Fullerton College, a local community college. She also got a job at a perfume and makeup counter at The Broadway department store and thought about becoming a makeup artist.

And she was still having fun with No Doubt. To promote the band, Gwen and a friend bought as many children's extra-large T-shirts and tank tops as they could find at inexpensive stores. They printed pink No Doubt logos on the shirts. Then they sold them at concerts.

In the summer of 1989, No Doubt played its first out-of-state show in Arizona. Only about a hundred people came to the show, but the band was excited anyway. Over the next two years, the band continued to perform throughout the Los Angeles area.

In August 1991, an executive from Interscope Records attended a No Doubt concert. The band was thrilled when they were offered their first recording contract. They immediately began work on their first album, *No Doubt*.

Interscope Records founder Jimmy Iovine had a feeling about the band—especially twenty-two-year-old Gwen. He recognized her star qualities, her talent, and her charisma. He assured her that she'd be a star in five years.

Gwen didn't see it. "Yeah, right," she thought to herself. "First off, I won't be with my band then; second, I'll have, like, five kids, and third, there's just no way."

In the early 1990s, No Doubt had many enthusiastic fans at California universities. Here the band performs at the University of California–Irvine.

Chapter **THREE**

THE BIG TIME

THE BAND RELEASED THEIR UPBEAT, SKA-INFLUENCED
first album, *No Doubt*, in March of 1992. But they
didn't get the radio play they wanted.

"It would take an act of God for this band to get on
the radio," said the program director of KROQ radio,
a major Los Angeles station. No Doubt had hoped
their music would be played on the station. But
grunge music was popular at the time, and bands like
Nirvana and Pearl Jam were filling the airwaves.
Radio DJs didn't think there was room for No Doubt's
ska sound. The band members tried not to get dis-
couraged and continued working hard at their day
jobs. Gwen still had her job at the makeup counter,
and Tony had started working as a salesperson at The

Broadway too. Tom ran a music equipment rental business. Adrian worked as a waiter at a steakhouse.

In the fall, No Doubt was excited to go on its first national tour. For two and a half months, the band members toured the country in vans. They opened for bands such as Public Enemy and The Special Beat. The excitement of performing live and the applause fired up the band.

In March 1993, they began work on their second album, which they planned to call *Tragic Kingdom*. Over the next two and a half years, the band recorded the album piece by piece in eleven different recording studios.

While working on *Tragic Kingdom*, tension formed between Gwen and her brother Eric. In many ways, Eric had been the driving force behind the band. Things were changing. Gwen, more than anyone else in the band, was popular with the concert crowds. Her confidence soared. "Gwen used to say that Eric, always a talented cartoonist, invented her," wrote Chris Heath of *Rolling Stone*. Heath noted how, over time, Gwen had evolved as an artist. She became more confident and in charge of her career. In a sense, she became something different from "Eric's creation." "And people seemed to like this new Gwen. Part of him was happy for her, but part of him was jealous," Heath added.

In 1994 Eric Stefani decided to quit the band and become an animator for *The Simpsons*. Gwen was upset.

She and Eric hadn't been getting along, but she didn't want him to leave the band. Gwen and Eric's parents encouraged them to go into therapy together to work out their problems. Over time they mended their relationship. Gwen credits Eric for inspiring her to be a serious musician. She appreciates everything she learned from him about how to be in a band and how to write songs.

Gwen faced another big change that year. After a seven-year relationship, Tony broke up with her. She didn't understand why. Her heart was shattered. For comfort she turned to music. But it was difficult to be around Tony when the band rehearsed and performed.

Gwen respects her brother Eric (left) *for having great confidence in her during her early years as a musician.*

She wasn't ready to see him dating anyone else. She also found it hurtful to spend so much time with Tony without getting to act like his girlfriend. "How can we hang out each day, and I can't touch you?" she remembered of the challenging time. "And that's why we stayed together for such a long time: because he was such a good friend to me that he could never hurt me. Even though he was already killing me, just by me knowing he didn't want to be with me."

Even though it was painful, Gwen and Tony managed to remain friends. They were devoted to the band and didn't want to get in the way of its success. Gwen later reflected that they both knew it was worth it to keep going with No Doubt.

BLOSSOMING SONGWRITER

Gwen's breakup pushed her to look deeper within herself for courage and talent. Gwen felt that while she was dating Tony she had been dependent on him for her happiness. She poured her emotions into heartfelt song lyrics. She discovered her talent as a songwriter and composed some of her strongest pieces, including "Sunday Morning," "Spiderwebs," and "Don't Speak." "Once I knew I could write songs, I blossomed," Gwen reflected. "It was like, power. Suddenly you don't have to be dependent on anyone else for happiness 'cause you've got this thing you can do."

Even though Tony had been the person to end the relationship, he sometimes found it hard to listen to

Gwen's songs about the breakup. But because he still loved Gwen, as a friend, he was happy for her. She was discovering her extraordinary creative talent.

TRAGIC KINGDOM AND MAGIC ON TOUR

In early 1995, No Doubt independently released an album of B-sides from *Tragic Kingdom*, called *The Beacon Street Collection*. The album was named after the house on Beacon Street in Anaheim where the band recorded their first songs in the garage studio. Originally, the record was sold only at concerts and local stores. The first thousand CDs sold out as the band toured to support the upcoming *Tragic Kingdom* release.

After more than two years of hard work and personal struggles, *Tragic Kingdom* was released later that year. The album was a mixture of new wave, pop, punk, rock, and ska music. One song on the album was instantly a hit. "Just a Girl," written by Tom and Gwen, launched the band onto radio waves and into living rooms and dance clubs across the country. The album had other hits too, such as "Spiderwebs" and "Hey You." Gwen's gut-felt heartbreak song, "Don't Speak," was a favorite among fans. Within months No Doubt had several singles at the top of the *Billboard* charts.

Interscope Records arranged for No Doubt to go on tour with another band on the record label, the British alternative rock band Bush. The leader of the band, Gavin Rossdale, was a tall, handsome singer and guitarist. When No Doubt first heard that the band was to perform with Bush, the band members weren't happy about it. Bush played a different kind of music than they did.

"The label was always talking about *Gavin and Bush*," remembered Gwen, who had been unimpressed at the time. "We were just like, 'Whatever. We are not going on tour with those guys; that's not what we are.'"

Despite the band's hesitation, the record label pushed the idea forward. No Doubt and Bush soon performed together at a club in Los Angeles. There, Gwen and Gavin met for the first time. "It was magic," Gwen recalled.

Gavin took an immediate liking to Gwen. "The first thing he said to me was, 'You're gorgeous,'" she remembered. But she needed more persuasion. She was still getting over Tony, and she didn't imagine herself dating a famous, good-looking musician like Gavin. She explained, "I'm usually attracted to guys with good personalities, ones that make me laugh." Nevertheless, she agreed when he asked her out. The two hit it off. They were soon an item.

Guys in the band felt protective of Gwen. They didn't trust Rossdale. He was a handsome rock star with many adoring female fans. They didn't want Gwen to get hurt.

"It was a very crazy time," explained Gwen. "There was already my breakup with Tony, and we were enjoying our success for the first time and [dealing with] having outside things come in to our little band, our little family. And then I met Gavin. It was really

Gwen and Bush leader Gavin Rossdale posed for this publicity shot during their tour stop at the 1995 Santa Barbara Bowl.

lonely, because I felt like nobody wanted me to go out with him. My ex-boyfriend and all of my, like, brothers in the band were saying, 'You are not gonna go out with that guy!'"

When Gavin and Gwen first met, they weren't crazy about each other's music. Gavin was a fan of only one No Doubt song, and Gwen wasn't very interested in his style of rock music. But as they got to know each other better, that changed. Gwen became a big fan of Gavin's music because she appreciated his talent, poetry, and writing. In turn, her music grew on Gavin too.

PLATINUM

The band's newfound fame kept increasing. In early 1996, No Doubt made their late-night TV debut with performances on *Late Night with Conan O'Brien* and *The Late Show* with David Letterman. They continued opening for Bush on tour. They played a half-hour set each night. Even when Gwen broke her foot during a performance in May, the tour continued with Gwen's foot on the mend.

By July *Tragic Kingdom* had gone platinum, selling a million records in less than a year. Around the same time, Gwen herself went platinum—she dyed her dark-blonde hair platinum blonde. The album was certified double-platinum in just another month.

After performing "Don't Speak" and "Excuse Me Mr." on *Saturday Night Live* in December, the band rock-

Tom Dumont (left) *and Tony Kanal* (right) *rock out at a 1996 performance in Mountain View, California. The band was in the early weeks of the* Tragic Kingdom *tour.*

eted into even more fame. *Tragic Kingdom* reached number one on the *Billboard* chart. The media focused mostly on Gwen. Her smiling face appeared on magazine covers on newsstands everywhere. Teen fashion magazines wrote about Gwen's unique, sometimes outrageous, style. Girls across the country copied her funky outfits.

In February 1997, the band was thrilled to attend the Grammy Awards. They performed their hit "Spiderwebs" at the live award program. No Doubt was nominated for two Grammys, Best Rock Album and Best New Artist. They didn't win any awards that night, but they were happy to be nominated. Later that year, their video for "Don't Speak" was honored with the Best Group Video award at the MTV Video Music Awards.

No Doubt took time off to relax in early 1998. The band members also took time to enjoy their newfound wealth. No longer starving artists, they all moved into new homes, moving from Anaheim to Los Angeles. They also rented a home in the Hollywood Hills to use as their recording studio. They began penning songs for their next album. They tried to balance their time between writing new music and making public appearances to promote the band. In March, Gwen took home a California Music Award statue for Outstanding Female Vocalist Statewide. No Doubt won the award for Outstanding Group Statewide.

Gwen's new blue look included lots of sparkly stick-on jewels.

The band attended the MTV Video Music Awards in September. Gwen made a splash with a bold new look. Her hair, tied up in little buns, was dyed the same shade of blue as the fuzzy, bright blue bra top she wore.

The band had some fun that fall when they recorded "I Throw My Toys Around" with Elvis Costello for *The Rugrats Movie* soundtrack. Costello cowrote the song with his wife, jazz singer and pianist Diana Krall, specially for the movie. The soundtrack was released in November.

No Doubt stayed busy with various creative projects and public appearances. But they continued to pour their hearts into writing songs for their upcoming album. As each song took shape, the band grew more and more excited. At the end of December, No Doubt celebrated a great year by throwing a big New Year's Eve party at Gwen's Los Angeles home. Ben Stiller, the Red Hot Chili Peppers, Tommy Lee, Beck, and other celebrities attended the event and partied well into the first hours of 1999.

ACCIDENTS HAPPEN

ne day Gwen was working on a song with the band in the studio. She sang her vocals over and over again to get them just right, while producers and sound mixers worked on the track. Gwen was concentrating so hard on her work that she didn't notice her fourteen-year-old dog, Maggen, had had an accident on the recording studio carpet. When Gwen saw what Maggen had done, she quickly cleaned up the mess with paper towels. Then she ran to the garbage bin area just outside the studio to throw the mess away. Unfortunately, the door to the gated trash area slammed behind her and locked her in—with the stinky garbage. "There I am, standing on top of the garbage bin that smells awful while everyone is inside a sound-proof studio!" laughed Gwen.

After the celebration, the band's successful streak continued into the new year. In March, the band received the Recording Industry Association of America's (RIAA) Diamond Award for *Tragic Kingdom*. The Diamond Award is an honor bestowed on albums that have sold over ten million copies in the United States.

The band spent that spring in the studio, recording tracks for their new release. They didn't have a name for the album yet, but they figured a title would come to them. They had been working on the project for well over a year. They were pleased with their album's new sound, a fusion of 1980s New Wave music, rock, pop, and reggae.

"Ex-Girlfriend"

Although Gwen had become a superstar, Gavin's popularity with his female fans still made her nervous. Gwen sometimes wished she "had a little leash" to keep Gavin close to her. Unfortunately, that wasn't possible. Gavin had a house in London and was usually on tour with his band. The couple managed to spend about six months of the year together. Gwen was busy with touring and songwriting for No Doubt's next album, but she missed Gavin and wished he lived closer. Other things were hard on the relationship too.

Gavin was a private person and didn't like the fact that Gwen talked about their relationship with the press. He also disliked the way Gwen wrote about their personal lives and his romantic past in the lyrics of her songs. For example, the album that No Doubt had in the works included the song "Ex-Girlfriend," about a former girlfriend of Gavin's. He didn't want his private and personal life to become public information. The pressures of their relationship became too much for the pair. Gavin and Gwen broke up.

For the next several months, the band continued working on the album. They wanted it to be perfect. They took a break from recording in September to launch an eight-city West Coast tour to promote their forthcoming album. Gwen sported a new look for the tour. She dyed her hair bright bubblegum pink. However, despite her cheerful hair color, inside Gwen felt anything but happy.

A reporter later asked Gwen why she dyed her hair

such a flamboyant color. "Because that's what you do when you break up with someone," she replied. "I look at it [in retrospect] and I go 'uccch,' but it so perfectly reflects exactly where I was, which was very unsure of myself."

On October 3, Gwen turned thirty. Her life felt topsy-turvy. While she was thrilled about the upcoming album, she was heartsick about her breakup with Gavin. But she thought that the lyrics she had written for No Doubt's new songs were the best she'd ever written. Gwen knew that her life and career weren't slowing down and that she didn't have time to be depressed for long. She focused her energy on her music and her fans.

Later that year, the band was excited to win the award for Most Stylish Video—for the song "New"—at the VH1/Vogue Fashion Awards. Gwen was also nominated for Most Fashionable Female Artist, though she didn't win. Looking uniquely stylish as always, she showed off new multicolored braces at the event.

The new album was on the verge of being born, and on December 31, 1999, No Doubt rang in the new millennium with a bang. They played at the MTV New Year's Eve celebration in Times Square. The band went onstage just after midnight and performed "It's the End of the World As We Know It (And I Feel Fine)" by REM. They also revived their old hit "Spiderwebs." And in the worldwide-televised performance, No Doubt performed their upcoming single, "Ex-Girlfriend."

The next month, "Ex-Girlfriend" hit stores. Fans rushed out to buy the single and downloaded it off the Internet. The song quickly jumped to the top of the alternative radio charts.

The press asked Gwen and the other band members if the song was about Gwen and Gavin's breakup. The band explained that the song was about Gwen and Gavin—but not their breakup. The ex-girlfriend in the lyrics referred to an anonymous former love of Gavin's.

RETURN OF SATURN

Finally, in April 2000, the band's much-anticipated album *Return of Saturn* was released. In one week, it shot to number two on the *Billboard* Top 200. "It's a selfish record in a way," Gwen admitted to the press, "because the songs are largely about me and my insecurities. I laid it all out there, and it feels good."

While Gwen's career soared to new heights, things were looking up in her personal life too. Gavin and Gwen worked things out and reunited during the spring of 2000. As an artist, Gwen needed to be able to express her inner thoughts and feelings through her music. But she stopped talking to reporters about the personal details of her relationship. Later that year, the music video for the song "Simple Kind of Life" featured her running happily in a wedding dress, singing about her longtime desire to be a wife and mother.

In 2000 and 2001, Gwen made guest appearances on two other artists' hit singles. In November 2000, the eclectic techno-musician Moby released a version of his song "South Side" featuring Gwen. The song swiftly climbed the charts. The next year, Gwen was heard on rapper Eve's hit single "Let Me Blow Ya Mind." One writer noted the similarities between Eve and Gwen. "Like Stefani, [Eve] balances her sex appeal with smart songs about independence and self-worth." Gwen's collaborations with other artists showed the music world that she possessed great versatility as an artist—versatility that she would continue to explore in future projects.

COSMIC TITLE

The title *Return of Saturn* refers to an astrological event. About every thirty years from a person's birth, the planet Saturn completes an orbit around the sun. It returns to the same position it was in when that person was born. In astrology, a person is said to experience their "Saturn return" between the ages of twenty-eight and thirty— Gwen's age as No Doubt was writing and recording the album. This period is often associated with emotional upheaval, challenges, reflection, and change. The band members recognized those themes on their new album as they settled on a title for it.

Stefani shows off her Rock Steady tour jeans in a No Doubt performance at the 2001 My VH1 Video Awards.

Chapter **FOUR**

ROCK STEADY

IN **2001** NO DOUBT RELEASED *ROCK STEADY,* A different kind of album. On past albums, the band members had worked only with one another. On *Rock Steady*, they worked with several talented people in the recording industry, such as singer-songwriter Bjork and the Eurythmics' producer Dave Stewart.

"That was a really big step for us," said Stefani. "Because we never really let anyone into the family before." She felt more pressure also because they were working with such big-name musicians. She had idolized Dave Stewart and the Eurythmics when she was growing up. Her admiration for Stewart pushed her extra hard to perform well on the album.

Stefani wanted to record an album that would be fun to dance to. The band had recently been inspired by dance hall music. "You've got this really simple music, but it's so infectious," said Stefani. She added that they had been going to dance clubs frequently and wanted to record music that would be played in the clubs.

"Hey Baby," a song about the groupies (fans) who flirt with the male band members, was an instant hit. Critics raved about the new album. "[*Rock Steady* is] a mix of classic New Wave sounds, hard-driving hip-hop beats and slinky Jamaican dancehall," said a writer for New York's *Daily News* in 2001.

Taking a break from promoting their new album, the band members headed back to the recording studio. They recorded a remixed version of disco legend Donna Summer's 1975 hit, "Love to Love you Baby." The song was for the soundtrack of the film *Zoolander*, released in September 2001. The comedy starred No Doubt's friend Ben Stiller, who played a fashion model.

Besides making music, No Doubt focused their creative forces on making music videos. In the 2002 video for the hit "Underneath It All," a song about Stefani's romantic happiness, Stefani made a rare kind of appearance—bare faced. For once, she wasn't wearing her trademark red lipstick and heavy mascara. The lyrics of that song, which spoke to Stefani's "real Prince Charming," were written for Gavin.

Stefani and her bandmates found a unique way to promote their new album. Appearing unannounced at a

California high school, No Doubt performed songs from *Rock Steady* to an auditorium full of awestruck students. MTV Productions filmed the whole thing. Before the show, Stefani and the band had fun surprising students, many of them huge No Doubt fans.

Stefani had a way of connecting with young people. They were drawn to her exciting, fun personality. But most of all, they appreciated her talent as a musician and songwriter. "I LOVE singing to her songs," said Alanna Donovan, a fan from Ohio. "They are really empowering to women who want to feel good. Then again, she has also written some really great breakup songs. They are good to listen to when you have had your heart broken."

Fans liked the new No Doubt sound too. In December 2001, *Rock Steady* debuted in the top ten on album sales charts. The band was thrilled with the success of their album. They were on a winning streak. "Our egos were gone," said Stefani of her bandmates. "We were just so in love with each other and so proud of the album. It was like, 'This is crazy, how'd we get so far?'"

"MARRY ME"

Several weeks later, Stefani had a very happy new year—she and Gavin got engaged on New Year's Day 2002. They planned to marry in September. The announcement wasn't a shock to friends and family. Gavin's dad, Richard Rossdale, had seen it coming. "They are a good couple," he said.

Others voiced similar confidence in the pair, especially since they had already been through so much together. "In a business where people get married after six weeks, they've been together six years," commented Stefani's friend Rachel Zoe Rosensweig. "That gave them time to develop a friendship. Another friend of Stefani's, Kendra Pahukoa, agreed. "It's the real deal."

Nine months later, on September 14, 2002, a bright-blue Rolls Royce pulled up in front of St. Paul's Covent Garden in London. Gwen Stefani, arriving an hour late to the ceremony, stepped out of the car in an elegant pink and white silk Christian Dior wedding gown designed by John Galliano.

Stefani held her father's arm as she walked down the aisle. She carried her mother's Catholic prayer book. Rossdale's escort was his beloved Hungarian sheepdog, Winston. "Gwen was choked with emotion. She cried, he cried—so did the dog!" said designer Galliano.

After the ceremony, everyone boarded double-decker buses to Home House, an exclusive club. Guests dined on a six-course Italian dinner, then danced into the night. Galliano commented that the whole event, including a choir, roses, and twinkling stars, was extremely romantic.

The couple flew to the beautiful Isle of Capri in Italy for their honeymoon. Two weeks later, Stefani put on her wedding dress again. She and Gavin got married a second time, this time in Los Angeles. Stefani joked, "That dress was the whole reason I had another wedding."

Gavin and Gwen seal their marriage with a kiss in London's Covent Garden.

But really, Stefani and Rossdale had a second ceremony and reception so that their family and friends—including then-couple Brad Pitt and Jennifer Aniston and actor Ben Stiller—could attend.

Stefani was thrilled to be married. Her love for Rossdale inspired her and filled her with creative energy. "He's the one who gets to me and turns on my feelings, and when my feelings are turned on, I can write songs. He's definitely my muse."

Stefani had a new last name too. When she married, she took her husband's last name. Legally, she is Gwen Rossdale. Her stage name remains Gwen Stefani.

GRAMMY GIRL

Stefani had more excitement and success in 2002. She was nominated for a Grammy Award for her 2001 collaboration with Eve on the rap hit "Let Me Blow Ya Mind." She had already won awards for her collaborations with both Eve and Moby at the September 2001 MTV Video Music Awards.

Stefani attended the Grammys with the other members of No Doubt. Sporting a sheer, leopard-print gown and high-heeled lace-up boots, she was overjoyed when she won her first Grammy award.

PUSHED TO THE LIMIT

One morning while eating breakfast, Stefani heard a song on the radio. The song was one of her favorite dance tunes from the 1980s—Club Nouveau's "Why You Treat Me So Bad." Stefani had an idea. She told Tony Kanal that she wanted to do a version of the song. Kanal thought it was a great idea.

She might even want to put out a solo record, she thought. She mentioned the idea to Jimmy Iovine at Interscope. But for then, the project would have to wait. After all, she was in the middle of the 2002 *Rock Steady* tour, and her time and energy were pushed to the limit.

The tour, promoting the triple-platinum record, took the band all over the world between March and November. In the United States, they opened several shows for The Rolling Stones and performed with bands such as Garbage.

GWEN'S SELF-IMAGE

wen Stefani doesn't see herself the way her fans see her. She's modest, and her celebrity image doesn't sit very well with her.

"The fame, celebrity-sex symbol part of the whole thing is just always really odd, but also really flattering," says Stefani. "You never really picture yourself like that." Even so, she admits that she knows how to play up that image. "So the sex symbol part, I don't know about that. Good for me. It makes me laugh. And it makes me happy. Whatever." She jokes, "If only [fans] knew what a dork I really am."

While Stefani doesn't always understand her sex-symbol status, she sometimes enjoys the powerful effect she has on her fans. One day she was driving down Hollywood Boulevard in Los Angeles. She saw a young man of about nineteen walking down the sidewalk. He was wearing an old No Doubt T-shirt. Stefani figured he was a fan. She pulled up alongside him and rolled down her window. "Hey, cool shirt!" she shouted. His reaction: "The guy seriously nearly fell over. He totally tripped. It was so cute," recalls Stefani.

The long tour wore on No Doubt. Spending weeks on the road and performing in different cities every night was exhausting. Stefani and the rest of the band were relieved when the tour was finally over. They needed a break. They all wanted more time to relax, enjoy other creative endeavors, and spend time with their spouses and families. Stefani especially felt burned out.

But stepping back into ordinary life wasn't easy, either. "Reality becomes totally skewed [during a tour], but it's such an amazing time because you get lost in your own world," said Stefani. "That's what's so hard about coming off a tour. All of a sudden you go, Oh my God, I have to have keys. I have to have money in my purse. Someone is not going to do every single thing for me."

Over the next several months, as Stefani started to pursue a solo project, rumors spread through the press and across the Internet that No Doubt had broken up. However, she and the band denied those rumors, insisting that they were still together.

MEETING STING AGAIN

In 2003 No Doubt came together again to perform at the Super Bowl. Stefani was excited to perform with her longtime idol, Sting. During halftime, Stefani performed in a sequined bikini top and wrestling shoes and did push-ups on the stage. "How Sting kept his mind on his singing, I'll never know," commented a reporter.

Fortunately, Stefani's second time meeting Sting was a more positive experience than the first. After the show, she told Sting about meeting him years ago, backstage at a Police concert, when she was sixteen. "Oh man," Sting replied, "I was such a [jerk] then." Stefani admired him more than ever after that day.

Sting kissed Stefani's hand after performing his song, "Message in a Bottle," with No Doubt at the 2003 Super Bowl.

NO DOUBT REUNION

During 2003 No Doubt took a much-needed break and spent time with their loved ones. But by 2004, Stefani and the guys were eager to perform together once again. That summer Stefani hit the road with No Doubt, promoting their November 2003 release, *No Doubt: The Singles 1992–2003*.

Stefani worked hard to get her body in shape for the tour. She resumed training with weights and felt great about the strength she gained. She was thrilled to get back onstage with her old friends in No Doubt.

"It was so magical—to step out on stage and play for that many people who know all your songs," she said. The *Singles* album featured all of the band's top hits, so it was popular with No Doubt fans new and old. "And there's that instant gratification thing that happens when we play live," the singer added. "It's that bond between you and the audience."

Stefani joined Steven Tyler, lead singer of the rock band
Aerosmith, in a performance at the Rock and Roll Hall of Fame
in March 2003. That night, she welcomed one of her favorite
bands, The Police, into the Hall of Fame.

Chapter **FIVE**

LOVE. ANGEL.
MUSIC. BABY.

AFTER THE LONG, EXHAUSTING *ROCK STEADY* TOUR ended in late 2002, Stefani had been ready to lie low with her newlywed husband for a while. But there wasn't time. Her record label boss, Jimmy Iovine, wanted her to start writing songs. He knew that she was ready to begin work on a solo record. Iovine was extremely supportive of Stefani's solo project and took charge of it, pushing the singer to go for it. Pairing her with hit songwriter Linda Perry, Iovine encouraged Stefani to write.

At first Stefani was intimidated. She had never written songs with a complete stranger before. Perry wrote, "What You Waiting For," encouraging Stefani to go ahead with her own career—to see herself as a serious songwriter and solo performer.

"I think Gwen is very over-critical of herself," said Linda Perry. She recalled a day when Stefani had "a little insecurity breakdown." Perry saw it as a good sign that Stefani was not a conceited superstar. "I found it very endearing; I loved seeing her that insecure. You meet a lot of people who have half her talent and they think they're God's creative monster."

Studio Time

Once Perry and Stefani had written several songs, it was time for Stefani to work with others in the recording studio. "I cried before I went in the studio," she said. "I was just terrified."

"It was her first time doing something without her band, and it was a big step," said producer Iovine. Recognizing how nervous she was, he asked her to just try things out and see how it went.

Stefani was slated to work with some of the hottest people in the recording industry, such as hip-hop producers the Neptunes. Luckily an old friend had a hand in the project too—former boyfriend and No Doubt bandmate Tony Kanal. But Stefani wasn't used to having so many people giving her input on her work.

She said the experience was "horrifying" at first. Because songwriting is so personal for her, she initially found it hard to work with people she admired but barely knew. She missed the easy comfort she had with her friends of No Doubt. But over the next few months, Stefani grew comfortable working on the new

Record producers Pharrell Williams (left) *and Chad Hugo* (right) *call themselves the Neptunes. Together they produce hip-hop and pop music.*

record with a team of talented artists. On several tracks, she even shared vocals with popular artists such as Eve and Andre 3000.

For the first time, Stefani's husband also contributed to one of her projects, writing some of the lyrics for "The Real Thing." Rossdale helped with some of her creative decisions too. In Stefani's previous work with No Doubt, Rossdale didn't feel comfortable offering his musical input. He didn't want Stefani's bandmates to think he was interfering. "But when I'm on my own," Stefani reflected, "we can talk even more, he can have more of an opinion. It's been really . . . romantic."

When the record was completed, Stefani felt like something was still missing. "I was finished with the album, but I knew in my heart that I didn't have my attitude song," she said.

Just minutes later, Stefani and producer Pharrell Williams wrote "Hollaback Girl," a sassy song about a tough high school girl. Although the lyrics talk about fighting, for Stefani, the song was simply about being a strong person. (The singer says she never got into fights in high school.)

The record had taken a year of hard work to produce. When asked to describe the experience in five words, Stefani replied, "Creative. Draining. Intimidating. Exhilarating when the songs came. A year I'll never forget. How do you say that in one word?"

FLYING SOLO AND SOARING

After seventeen years of working with No Doubt, Gwen Stefani released her first solo album in November 2004. She was confident that her fans would enjoy *Love.Angel.Music.Baby.* "The thing about my record is you can try to not like it," Stefani remarked. "But you know what? It's gonna be your guilty pleasure. I just know it!"

The album quickly climbed up the *Billboard* charts and MTV video ratings. It created six hit singles and videos. The megahit "Hollaback Girl" soon became the top-selling legal digital download in history.

Fans and music critics raved about the record, which sold over seven million copies worldwide. "[Stefani] has proved to possess a Madonna-like versatility in her ability to successfully tackle numerous contemporary styles," said Chuck Taylor of *Billboard* magazine. "The fifth single ('Luxurious') . . . [serves] a chillin' beat and beefy R&B vocal.

"['Crash'] returns the pop princess to her sing-songy nursery school persona . . . but as juvenile as "Crash" is,

Stefani staged an elaborate performance of "What You Waiting For" at the American Music Awards in November 2004.

it is also clever and catchy," added Taylor. "Warning: impossible to dislodge from the brain once inserted."

In the hit tune "Cool," written with Dallas Austin, Stefani shared her personal life with fans once again. The song had a double meaning. It was partly about letting go of her exclusive working relationship with No Doubt. The lyrics also spoke of her breakup with Tony Kanal and how they have a lasting friendship. In the song, Stefani sings about being happy after everything they've been through, they're still "cool.'"

TOUGH CRITICS

The new album, showcasing dance tunes, hip-hop beats, and a range of artists, appealed to a large audience. But some listeners missed the special chemistry Stefani had with No Doubt.

"When I saw [No Doubt] live, I remember her energy just pulsating with her band and it was magic," said a fan. "[Her solo album] seemed to lack that heart that she had with No Doubt." Some fans also missed the rock element of No Doubt's music. A critic from *USA Today* pointed out how frequently the word "girl" appeared in song titles on the album (three times). She called the music "fun, fizzy, frivolous."

Stefani defended her new record. "I didn't feel like I had to make something that was serious. If you listen to the lyrics and music," she said, "it's not a serious album! It's just pure fun."

Stefani created an award-winning video for the hit single "Hollaback Girl." The video featured a special appearance by cheerleaders from California's Orange Crush All-Stars Open Team. Some people criticized the fact that Stefani, a woman in her mid-thirties, was performing with teenagers.

"Someone should tell her that . . . shaking some pompoms and hanging around a bunch of high-school girls makes her look like just a delusional older woman," chided a young man in a letter to *Flare* magazine.

STEFANI'S HARAJUKU GIRLS

A group of stylish Japanese teenagers gave Gwen Stefani special inspiration on her first solo album. Stefani wanted to dedicate one song on *Love.Angel.Music.Baby.* to the girls she admired while visiting Tokyo's Harajuku shopping area. She recognized their innovative ensembles as "self-expression through fashion." she particularly liked the way their style reflected both Eastern and Western cultures and the ideas that each had adopted from the other.

The wild personal style of people in the Harajuku neighborhood fascinated Stefani, especially as she watched it change over time. "The last couple of times I was there," she recalled in early 2005, "it had evolved into all these different things like the Gothic Lolitas and these [Japanese] girls with blonde hair and dark tans and high-heel shoes, like they were from

Two Japanese girls show off their style in the Harajuku district of Tokyo. Popular 2004 styles included Gothic Lolita (left) *and traditional kimono with lighthearted cat-ear headbands* (right).

Hollywood." Stefani decided to add four Harajuku-styled dancers to her act. Soon the Harajuku girls were appearing with Stefani on her album art, tour, and in public appearances and videos.

Not everyone appreciated the addition to Stefani's act. Some people think that the Harajuku girls perpetuate negative stereotypes about Asian women. Writer MiHi Ahn reported on *Salon.com*, "In interviews, [the Harajuku girls] silently vogue in the background like living props. . . . They're ever present in her videos and performances—swabbing the deck aboard the pirate ship, squatting gangsta style in a high school gym while pumping their butts up and down, simpering behind fluttering hands or bowing to Stefani." Criticizing the singer, Ahn continued, "She's taken Tokyo hipsters . . . and turned them into China dolls."

Stefani took the Harajuku theme more lightly. She could relate to the girls of the Harajuku neighborhood and their hip style. Like her, the girls expressed themselves—their personalities and their enthusiasm for life—through their clothing.

MOVIE QUEEN

"I went crazy-nuts when I heard I had gotten the part," said Stefani of her role as Hollywood legend Jean Harlow in the 2004 release *The Aviator*. The movie, directed by famous filmmaker Martin Scorsese, starred Leonardo DiCaprio as millionaire Howard Hughes. The film also featured Jude Law and Cate Blanchett.

The minor role of Jean Harlow was perfect for Stefani, who had loved old movies and Hollywood glamour since childhood. Even though her part in the film was small, she prepared hard for the role. She went out to the video store and rented every Jean Harlow movie that she could find.

As Stefani researched the movies and life of Jean Harlow, she became more and more inspired. "She was beautiful and sexy and one of the most creative women that I've ever known of. And her sense of fashion was light years beyond her time."

In Stefani's scene, Jean Harlow and Howard Hughes attend the premiere of Harlow's movie, *Hell's Angels*. Stefani marveled at the movie set and how realistic the scene felt—with five hundred extras as adoring Harlow fans. "So, in the scene we get out of the car and we are walking down the red carpet, and let me tell you that there was just no acting involved there. Everything was so real; it all felt so real."

For her role, Stefani wore $1 million worth of dazzling vintage diamond jewelry. Critics agreed that she wore it well. "Cast as Jean Harlow . . . Gwen swans through an onscreen film premiere as if she had been born wearing diamonds, white satin and Leonardo DiCaprio on her arm," said a writer from the magazine *Harper's Bazaar*.

"It's a perfect fit," said makeup artist Darrell Redleaf. "Gwen's signature red lips, blonde bombshell hair and arched brows are old Hollywood."

Stefani joked about the media focusing on her role in the film. She thought it was funny to be getting so much attention for playing such a small part. But she was grateful for the opportunity to act in a major film with such a talented cast. Stefani enjoyed the experience and would like to keep acting. "I've been trying to do films for years," she said, "but it's hard to find the right roles."

Stefani attended the December 2004 premiere dressed in a pink floral evening gown designed by Vivienne Westwood and dazzling, vintage Neil Lane diamonds. She held her husband's arm on the red carpet. Showing off her dress, she said, "This looks like something Jean Harlow would wear, right?"

By the end of 2004, Gwen Stefani had become a successful singer, songwriter, and movie actress. She had other plans for herself too.

Stefani joined the film's star, Leonardo DiCaprio, at the premiere of The Aviator. *The film opened at Mann's Chinese Theater in Los Angeles, California.*

IS GWEN A COPYCAT?

n 2006 Madonna told a reporter that Gwen Stefani was a copycat. "She has totally ripped me off," said Madonna. "We work with a lot of the same people. She married a British man. She has blonde hair. She changes her fashion sense with each new single. She obviously wants to be me." Stefani has pop-star status, platinum-blonde hair, and a tendency to transform her look frequently. Because of this, she has jokingly been referred to as "the new Madonna" by publications such as *The Hollywood Reporter* and *People*.

Some also saw the 1980s music style of *Love.Angel.Music.Baby.* as another way in which Stefani was imitating her predecessor. "On [her] solo debut, Stefani . . . gets into the '80s dance-pop groove as if she were the Material Girl in her heyday," said one writer.

But other critics see a difference between Stefani's style and Madonna's. They say Madonna's transformations are too thought out and business driven. On the other hand, "Stefani is more akin to a mad teenager who just really likes clothes and will wear them all at once to prove it," said a reporter from *The Times* in London.

Like Madonna, Gwen Stefani is a trendsetter. One of her early signature styles, wearing bindis (forehead jewelry), was copied by girls everywhere. *Spin* magazine called Stefani "the nice Catholic girl who brought Indian forehead fashion to the mall." Even Madonna picked up on the Indian-adornment trend.

Gwen Stefani and Madonna have met, and Madonna and her husband have even invited Gwen and Gavin to dinner at their house. And despite the similarities between the two pop stars, Stefani definitely has a style all her own, created from many outside influences—including, yes, even the Material Girl.

Throughout her solo tour, Stefani featured her unique taste in fashion. She liked surprising costume contrasts, like a marching band jacket with sporty shorts and high heels.

Chapter SIX

FASHION DESIGNER

IN 2001, WHILE WORKING WITH EVE ON THE VIDEO for "Let Me Blow Ya Mind," Stefani was paired with a fashion stylist for the first time. A stylist is a person who works with someone to develop a new look or personal style. Stefani had her own strong sense of style. At first she didn't want a stylist. But she changed her mind when she met Andrea Lieberman.

"I felt like I met this ultra-cool, New York, Jewish version of myself," laughed Stefani. "And I knew right away that we clicked, and that I wanted to work with her. I just could tell that she was tuned into my weird taste."

Stefani was used to mixing and matching clothes from thrift stores in Orange County. She has been designing her own clothing since childhood, and she had created all her own performance costumes in the earlier years of No Doubt. For one concert, she might wear men's pajama bottoms and combat boots with a knit scarf wrapped around her neck—teamed with a tank top and wristbands. Stefani had also designed her Jamaican-style costumes for No Doubt's *Rock Steady* tour, inspired by the fashions she saw while recording the album in Jamaica. For one of her tour costumes, she wore a mesh top under a bikini top. She also wore black pants covered with graffiti that resembled the album's artwork.

But in addition to her funky, sporty style, Stefani is famous for her glamour. She may wear an elegant, 1930s-style evening gown and diamond jewelry to a fancy event. Lieberman was a good fit as Stefani's stylist because Stefani knew she understood the wide range of Stefani's eclectic fashion sense.

Lieberman worked with Stefani to tweak her look and give her a high-fashion edge. She also helped her to create the wild fashions she imagined.

Together, the two designed costumes for the *Love.Angel.Music.Baby.* album cover and the album's solo concert tour. Stefani loved the creative process of working with Lieberman. They had fun staying up all night brainstorming. They gathered ideas by watching old movies and tearing pages from magazines. In the end, Stefani felt that the album cover, the costumes, and other design elements perfectly reflected the sound of the album.

Some critics didn't like Stefani's new fashion creations. A writer for *Teen People* wrote in 2005, "The style icon is severely out of tune in a microscopic plaid miniskirt with white tights, a belly-baring top, lace gloves and strap-happy platforms."

But Stefani tries not to take bad reviews too seriously. "It's not like it ever discourages me from doing something I want to do," she said. "If I followed what people said I should do, I wouldn't be here right now."

Stefani credits her "team," clothing stylist Andrea Lieberman and hair stylist Danilo, for helping her pull off her many looks. It takes Lieberman and Danilo about two hours to prepare Stefani for a photo shoot or red-carpet appearance such as an award show.

While Stefani likes to try out new looks and styles, she often goes back to the standards that she always liked. "I look back on the costumes I made for myself before anybody helped me out," she reflected, "when it was just my mom and me, fabric-shopping. And what's weird is that I'm wearing the same kind of thing I always wore. You keep repeating yourself. Well, I do—but in a mature, evolving way."

One day Stefani and Lieberman were talking about how many outfits they had made. They joked that they should create a clothing line together. But then they thought about it seriously. Singers Sean Combs, Beyonce, and Jennifer Lopez all had clothing lines. Gwen Stefani should have a line too. After all, she is known for her unique fashion sense, and she had years of experience designing her own costumes.

At first Stefani and Lieberman planned to launch just a small fashion line. They would sell their clothing and accessories in small boutiques. "And then I met this guy who said he wanted to do a clothing line with me and pay for everything," said Stefani. "The best part was he said I could do whatever I wanted creatively. I was like, are you kidding me? Okay."

Stefani decided to name her clothing line "L.A.M.B." in honor of Lamb, her beloved childhood dog. She liked the idea of remembering her dog through her clothing line. L.A.M.B. also stands for the first letter of each word in the title of her first solo album, *Love.Angel.Music.Baby.*

In 2003 the first L.A.M.B. products went on the market—a line of Le Sportsac bags. In the following months, the line branched into clothing and other accessories, although it didn't yet hit fashion runways.

Even when Stefani was working on her solo album, making public appearances, and preparing for her first solo concert tour, she was planning and sketching L.A.M.B. designs. She drew inspiration from some of her favorite brands in thinking up her own creations. "There were a lot of Japanese lines, like Super Lovers and Hysteric Glamour, that had this cute, casual thing I wanted L.A.M.B. to have," she explained.

Stefani understands why a number of musical artists have developed fashion lines. "Designing is an exten-

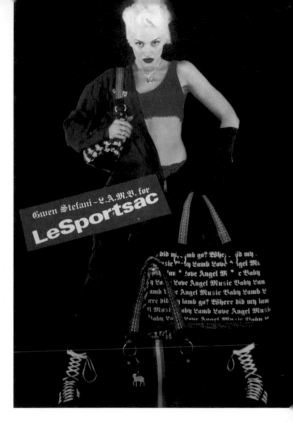

Le Sportsac's L.A.M.B. line featured the words "Love Angel Music Baby" printed on bags and purses.

sion of your personality," she said. "It comes from inside you. Visuals are just an extension of writing music and singing and dancing onstage." She's not put off by having to share the clothing industry with other musicians-turned-designers, though. After years of creating clothes for herself, she sees her clothing line as a new long-term career that she wants to pursue seriously. "Long after I'm too old to do cartwheels onstage, I'll be making clothes. I want to be making clothes forever," she said in 2005.

Stefani says that her music and her design ideas often influence each other. Of the two, design may be the more self-indulgent line of work for her. "Designing is just so fulfilling in a very selfish, greedy way," she gushed, "where I'm wondering what I can wear next, and I think it up and get to wear it."

Some people criticized Stefani's designs. They said the L.A.M.B. clothing wasn't easy for an ordinary woman to wear. Most women couldn't pull off the right look in the clothing, they said, without the accessories Stefani is known for: "a washboard stomach, a serious peroxide habit and rock-star arm-candy," referring to her heartthrob husband.

Other critics disagreed. Sally Springer of *Vogue* magazine called Stefani's designs "terrifically original and inspirational to women of varying ages."

Stefani's L.A.M.B. line released a very different kind of creation in May 2005: a digital camera. Stefani designed the exterior, while the camera itself was made by Hewlett-Packard. The stylish blue camera even had a built-in "help wizard" to help users take quality photos.

In July Stefani partnered with Royal Elastics to produce a line of L.A.M.B. sneakers. The shoes were available in four styles: Love, Angel, Music, and Baby. They were made of leather (in Love's case, gold leather) or canvas, and some were decorated with lyrics to Stefani's songs. Celebrities such as Lucy Liu and Cameron Diaz were spotted sporting the comfortable, sassy shoes.

Runway Magic

In September 2005, after two years of being in business, Stefani's L.A.M.B. clothing line made its runway debut at New York Fashion Week. The singer-designer explained that she had wanted to wait until the line was truly ready.

Stefani's main inspirations for the show were British royalty, English schoolboy uniforms, and the costumes from the hit movie *Pirates of the Caribbean*. The funky fashion line featured styles such as a black leather, military-style jacket, a tweed jacket and miniskirt, and a gothic-print cape. The show ended with a wedding dress, decorated with rhinestones that Stefani sewed on herself. "I'm very, very hands-on," she told a reporter.

Four days before the show, Stefani met with her codesigner on the fall line, Zaldy Goco, and her design assistants. She wanted to make sure that everything was organized, prepared, and ready for her show. "[Stefani's] clear about what she wants to see," said Zaldy, "and it makes it really easy for me to translate her vision."

At the show, Stefani honored her mother, Patricia, in her welcoming speech. She credited her mother for teaching her to sew. Stefani was happy to have her mom as her special guest that night.

The runway debut was a star-studded event. It featured supermodel Naomi Campbell on the runway. Rock star Lenny Kravitz and country singer Faith Hill sat in the front row with their young daughters. Many other famous people, including Britain's Sarah Ferguson, Diddy, Ashanti, Nicky Hilton, and Bijou Phillips, also attended.

Supermodel Naomi Campbell models one of Stefani's designs at the L.A.M.B. show at New York Fashion Week.

Stefani's biggest fan, Gavin, proudly watched his wife's first runway show. "It looked like [Gwen] coming down the catwalk over and over," said Rossdale. "She's really focused and knows what's in her mind and her vision. It's shocking, stunning."

The media also weighed in positively on the star's runway debut. "Staying true to her iconic rocker-turned-designer persona, Stefani's presentation was pure pop-video chic," said a *Flare* magazine writer. While a blend of music played—*The Sound of Music* soundtrack coupled with music from *Love.Angel.Music.Baby.*—models strutted down the stage in both classic evening gowns and street-smart sweatsuits. Silver sparkles, scattered on the runway, put the final touch on the glittery presentation. A reviewer from *People* sized up the show this way: "Part rasta, part rock and roll, part athletic wear and part glamour girl, her spring line is for the coolest tomboy in town."

STEFANI IS A STEPMOM

In October 2005, the press created another stir about Stefani for a very different reason. Tabloid newspapers reported that Gavin Rossdale, Stefani's husband of three years, had fathered a daughter in the late 1980s. The child's name was Daisy Lowe. Rossdale confirmed to the press that it was true but made no further comment.

Daisy's mother, Pearl Lowe, is a designer and singer in London. Gavin and Pearl had met as teenagers in England and had a brief relationship. Pearl had reportedly requested DNA tests because she had always wondered who Daisy's father was. When Pearl gave birth to Daisy, she asked Gavin to be the baby's godfather. A businessman named Bronner Lowe was named as the baby's father on the birth certificate. Daisy is an aspiring model.

Some newspapers reported that Gavin had always denied having any kind of relations with the child's mother and that Stefani was devastated by the news. Stefani told people not to believe what they read.

"They are dealing with this between the two of them," said a friend of the couple. "But it hasn't ruined the relationship, ruined the marriage. Gwen and Gavin remain very, very committed."

Stefani's reluctance to comment on her husband in interviews reflected that commitment. "I don't even like to talk about him because I've gotten into so much trouble mentioning him in my interviews. Our marriage is so sacred that the idea of sharing it with the world, and people judging it, is just gross."

HURRICANE RELIEF

Also during that fall, Stefani and many other stars worked together to benefit the victims of Hurricanes Katrina and Rita. Those storms had caused devastating damage to the Gulf Coast of Louisiana, Mississippi, and other southern states in August and September. Dangerous winds blew out windows and knocked down trees and power lines. Floodwaters breached the levees in New Orleans. Extensive flood damage from the hurricanes made countless homes unlivable. Residents of the affected areas needed massive amounts of aid to help their communities recover.

Many celebrities, including Stefani, wanted to find a way to help the victims. In early September, Stefani performed in the "Fashion Rocks" benefit concert at Radio City Music Hall. In November she appeared with stars from a number of record labels on a CD titled *Hurricane Relief: Come Together Now*. The two-disc album was released specially to raise money for relief organizations that were working in disaster areas. Musicians involved in the project didn't receive royalties (profits that artists make from the sale of the album). Instead, they donated all profits to the organizations helping to clean up, repair, and rebuild neighborhoods. Most of the money from the album's sales went to the American Red Cross, Habitat for Humanity, and MusiCares charities.

Stefani contributed to the CD on an all-new version of Eric Clapton's song "Tears in Heaven." She collaborated with Ringo Starr, Andrea Bocelli, and Mary J. Blige on the track. The album also featured Coldplay, Lenny Kravitz, Diddy, Norah Jones, John Mayer, Sting, Kanye West, Dave Matthews Band, and B.B. King, among many others.

"The creative community always responds to a tragedy," said Mitch Bainwol, chairman of the Recording Industry Association of America. "Everyone had the right attitude."

THE HARAJUKU LOVERS TOUR

Stefani's schedule was already busy, but she didn't want to disappoint her fans by taking time off. "I wasn't even going to go on tour, but then you guys kept buying the record, you kept tempting me," she jokingly told a reporter.

For two months, starting in late October 2005, Stefani switched gears from her clothing label to focus on the music of *Love.Angel.Music.Baby.* once again. Stefani, her crew, and the four Harajuku Girls hit the road, performing at arenas and stadiums across the country.

The first concert of the tour was in Anaheim, California—Stefani's hometown. Stefani was nervous. She had never toured without the comfort of her "brothers"

At the launch of the Harajuku Lovers Tour, Jimmy Iovine (right) *presented Stefani with an award for being the first artist in history to exceed one million digital downloads.*

in No Doubt. And she was especially nervous because the first show was in Anaheim. She didn't want to disappoint the crowd in her hometown.

But the star didn't need to worry about pleasing her fans. The spectacular Harajuku Lovers Tour show began with Stefani rising up out of the stage on a throne. Accompanied by a five-piece band, she then launched into the hit single "Harajuku Girls." During the number, the Harajuku dancers appeared. They accompanied Stefani throughout the show.

No Doubt fans who attended the show saw Stefani in a whole new light. "This tour is cheesy and girly and I love it," the singer said. "This is its own thing."

Throughout the show, Stefani changed costumes. During the song "Orange County Girl," she played up her sporty-casual style with a simple black tank top, black sneakers, and black and bright yellow pants. Behind her a huge video screen displayed old photos of Stefani from childhood to superstar status. While performing "Rich Girl," the singer was decked out in a pirate costume. Stefani transformed into a marching bandleader for her chart-topping song "Hollaback Girl."

Stefani considered the Harajuku Lovers Tour one of the hardest tour experiences of her life. She recalled pouring her energy into her electrifying shows night after night. When the concert ended each night, she'd go to her bus, collapse, and immediately fall asleep.

At the end of the tour in late December, Stefani told a reporter, "Come January, I'm just gonna hibernate and eat pizza and sleep."

A Secret is Revealed

On December 21, 2005, Stefani wrapped up her solo tour with a memorable moment at the Bank Atlantic Center, a concert stadium in a suburb of Fort Lauderdale, Florida. Her fans didn't know it at the time, but the singer was keeping a very big secret.

That evening, the concert was not going well for Stefani. She felt tired and burned out from the difficult tour. By the third song, she was short of breath. She gave a lackluster performance. The crowd felt her low energy.

Stefani knew she had to do something to save the show. During one song, she encouraged the audience to holler out. Unfortunately, she didn't get much of a reaction from the crowd. Stefani decided to pull out all the stops. She decided to reveal her secret to the Florida audience—and the world.

"I want you to do this so loud *the baby* hears you!" she yelled. The crowd went crazy. They screamed and whistled. They hadn't known that Stefani was pregnant.

After that final performance of the tour, tears rolled down Stefani's face. She hugged, kissed, and said good-bye to her musicians and backup dancers after the show. Her husband videotaped the tearful scene.

STYLIN' MOM-TO-BE

Being pregnant didn't put a stop to Stefani's sense of style. During her pregnancy, she especially liked roomy, kimono-inspired maternity dresses. They reflected the Japanese theme of her favorite fashions at the time.

Normally, Stefani's slim figure is part of her trademark style, and she is careful about her diet to maintain her weight. But while pregnant, she ate whatever she wanted, although she continued to work out. Instead of worrying about gaining weight, she wanted to make sure her body was getting enough nourishment. "It was worth it to have a healthy baby," she said of the 40 pounds she gained.

"I'm so sad, but I'm so glad it's over," said the four-month pregnant pop star. "I'm so glad." She was ready to take a break to fulfill her other dream, motherhood.

At the 2006 Grammy Awards, pop singer Bono (front left) *kissed Stefani's stomach and wished her and the baby well.*

Chapter SEVEN

HOME SWEET HOME

ON MAY 26, 2006, GWEN AND GAVIN announced the birth of their son, Kingston James McGregor Rossdale. The healthy baby boy weighed 7 pounds 8 ounces (about 3.4 kilograms) and had a full head of brown hair. Stefani's parents and husband were all present at the delivery. The next day, Rossdale assured the media that the new mom was doing very well. But because she had a cesarean (surgical) delivery, Stefani had to hold off on strenuous exercise for several weeks.

Kingston, the capital of Jamaica, was the main inspiration for baby Kingston's name. The music and fashions of Jamaica have always inspired Stefani. Kingston is also the name of a suburb near their London home.

DESIGNING IN NEW DIRECTIONS

In June 2006, Stefani introduced a line of baby fashions—Harajuku Lovers T-shirts, bibs, and onesies (one-piece sleepers). Stefani designed the baby fashion line to be "super kawaii [Japanese for *cute*]," as is everything about babies, in her opinion.

On September 15, 2006, Stefani launched her spring 2007 L.A.M.B. fashion line. During her second runway show, Stefani showcased animal print jackets, Guatemalan and Japanese prints, a neon green tie-dye print gown, and a bright red, sleeveless 1980s-style dress. The show also included shoes and handbags. Stefani found her inspiration for the show in the styles that actress Michele Pfeiffer wore in the 1970s and in the 1983 gangster movie *Scarface*.

Harajuku Lovers apparel included hats, shirts, and bibs featuring Japanese writing and cartoon characters.

HARAJUKU LOVERS

wen Stefani cares about her fans. So she wanted to create a line of clothing and accessories that were in financial reach of her younger fans. Stefani's Harajuku Lovers collection is more affordable than her expensive L.A.M.B. clothing line, designed for older, wealthier customers.

The casual, fun, Japanese-inspired clothes included T-shirts, hoodies, and tank tops—all printed with Stefani's lyrics and Japanese graphics. Stefani worked with a team of artists to create her designs. Some of the accessories featured illustrated characters inspired by the Harajuku Girls that accompanied Stefani on her *Love.Angel.Music.Baby.* album and tour.

The Harajuku Lovers line also included stationery and housewares. Items in the line could be purchased at smaller stores like Urban Outfitters and Hello Kitty, as well as large department stores such as Nordstrom and Barneys New York.

Meanwhile, Stefani worked on a unique item for the product line—a line of eight dolls called Love. Angel. Music. Baby. fashion dolls. Each 10-inch (25-centimeter) doll looks like Stefani or one of the Harajuku Girls in her act. Four of the limited-edition dolls show the singer in her various costumes, from "Bananas Gwen," in a marching band uniform, to "Tick-Tock Gwen," dressed as Alice in Wonderland. The dolls come with collectible items such as pocket mirrors, trading cards, and posters.

"Gwen Stefani has fulfilled every geeky girl's fantasy and turned herself from the woman at whose outfits the world scoffed to the designer whom fashionistas (fashionable people) strive to emulate," wrote a reporter from London's *The Times*.

Stefani wants to keep designing for the rest of her life. "My mom made all my clothes and her mom made hers, too," said Stefani. "It's definitely in my blood."

Stefani designed much of the show while she was pregnant. Because she was wearing comfortable maternity clothes at the time, she was inspired to design clothing that would be easy for women to wear.

The same month Stefani launched the spring clothing line, she also released a collection of canvas bags. The line of cute, creative bags included makeup cases and travel bags. According to Stefani, the artwork on the bags reflects "the whole world that was inside my head" while she was working on her first solo album. One white messenger bag is decorated with the words "Where did my lamb go?" scribbled repeatedly in Stefani's handwriting.

When Stefani tours, she trusts her talented staff of L.A.M.B. design assistants to run the business. She doesn't have time on tour to sit in on several-hour-long meetings that involve management or creative decisions.

The L.A.M.B. clothing line started as a line that included well-made, everyday clothes. Stefani wanted to create "cool jeans but ones that would make people say, 'Where did you get that? That's sick,'" she told *Vanity Fair*. Her next collection balanced the scope of the brand, featuring a variety of clothing from elegant gowns to super-short mini-dresses. Since L.A.M.B.'s runway debut, Stefani's line has even branched out to include costume jewelry made with metals and enamel.

Barbara Atkin, fashion director of Holt Renfrew (a high-end Canadian department store), believes that

Stefani discusses a new L.A.M.B. jacket with Andrea Lieberman (right) and another staff member at her New York studio before a fashion show in September 2006.

Stefani is a successful designer because "she's not taking street fashion and making it elitist. She's cleaning it up and giving it quality."

GWEN DRIVE AND GAVIN WAY

Also in September 2006, Stefani and her husband were happy to purchase a new home. The $15-million-dollar estate sits on two acres within The Summit, an exclusive, gated community that sits high in the hills of Los Angeles. The four-bedroom house was previously owned by singer and actress Jennifer Lopez. It will accommodate Gwen and Gavin's growing family—at 10,000 square feet, it is twice the size of their former

Gwen and Gavin play with Kingston in a park near their home in Primrose Hill, London.

home. The estate also features a swimming pool, basketball court, and tennis court.

Gwen and Gavin have another home in London's Primrose Hill neighborhood. And before relocating to The Summit, the couple had resided in the nearby Los Angeles neighborhood Los Feliz, in the mansion that Stefani had lived in since 1998. Their Los Feliz backyard was decorated with his-and-her street signs that read Gwen Drive and Gavin Way. Their driveway usually had one of their shiny Mercedes parked in it.

Stefani hates to do housework. Predictably—especially since the singer admits she is messy—her favorite perk of financial success is having a housekeeper. She concedes she would be "really, really, really bummed," if she ever lost that privilege.

Stefani also has a personal assistant, Pete, a former

schoolmate of Gavin's from England. Pete helps her with a variety of tasks—everything from planning her schedule to running errands and greeting guests.

In her free time—which is rare—Stefani likes to relax and be a regular person. She enjoys inviting friends over to her house to hang out. She also loves spending time with her husband or taking Kingston for walks in his stroller. "A great day for me is not getting out of bed. I like to see how many snacks I can eat there, how many crumbs I can drop, and how many really bad TV shows I can watch." She especially likes shows about babies being born and fashion makeovers. Stefani likes to listen to music too. Her musical tastes range from 1970s rock to 1980s new wave dance tunes to hip-hop. But she says she doesn't play CDs or records. Instead, she prefers listening to the radio.

Stefani is famous, but she's a real person too. She claims the only thing that sets her apart from most people is that she has "written a few songs and made a few clothes." She acknowledges that luck and a lot of talented people have helped her get where she is.

STEFANI'S GIGANTIC CLOSET

"I never thought I would be able to fill up a whole room with clothes," says Stefani in astonishment. Her housekeeper and assistant may top her list of favorite celebrity perks, but her closet can't be far behind. An entire room of her Los Feliz home was converted into a gigantic walk-in closet and filled to the brim with her clothing and accessories. It held everything from super-baggy pants and tight tanks to glamorous, slinky evening gowns. "I'm the luckiest girl in the world," she said of her giant closet.

About three-quarters of the clothing in the closet was designed by Stefani and her codesigners. Stefani is thrilled because she gets to keep all of the L.A.M.B. clothing samples (early designs from her shows). She provided the body size for all of her clothing samples, so all of the clothes fit her perfectly.

Even though she has a whole room full of clothing, Stefani often turns back to the basics, such as the comfy "Tanks a Lot" cotton tank top from her L.A.M.B. collection. Another favorite is her comfortable, well-worn pair of Levi's. She also gets a lot of wear out of her sweatsuits and her L.A.M.B. hoodies—especially "Lambie Cammi," a cashmere hoodie.

Her giant closet doesn't just have clothing from her own label. Stefani also collects clothing, shoes, boots, and handbags made by her favorite designers. These include Valentino, Versace, Prada, Alexander McQueen, Celine, Pierre Hardy, Jean Paul Gaultier, Louis Vuitton, and Vivienne Westwood. Stefani particularly likes Westwood's glamorous, timeless designs and has worn her gowns to many award shows. "I am a Vivienne Westwood maniac!" she gushes. "She is so magic!"

Stefani also collects Christian Dior (designed by Galliano) and John Galliano designs. She jokes that some of the dresses she has from Galliano's recent line remind her of Ice Capades costumes. She vows, "I will find an occasion to wear those, I can assure you."

"Everything in here makes it truly my dream closet," said Stefani. "Or at least it would be if it was a little bit better organized!"

BREAKING A SWEAT

To give herself energy for her many projects, Stefani sticks to a regular exercise routine. Staying in shape also fends off the insecurity and low self-esteem she feels when she's less fit. But being so thin and toned doesn't happen magically for her. "I want girls to know that I work at it—it's not easy, and it doesn't come naturally, unfortunately."

Although Stefani may be a trendsetter on the runway, she doesn't generally go for trendy workouts. "I'm old-school," says Stefani of her exercise habits. Running is her favorite form of exercise. She likes to break a sweat by jumping rope or running several days a week. While sometimes she has to force herself to work out, she loves how exercising makes her feel strong and vibrant. "Just now, after my workout, I was feelin' all tough and found myself thinking, Am I a man or a woman? I think that's a very creative way to feel."

Though she loves to eat pizza and sweets sometimes, Stefani prefers a healthy diet. She likes to eat a lean, low-carbohydrate diet of mostly fish and greens. Besides helping her have a muscular body, her healthy diet contributes to her radiant skin and glossy hair.

Stefani's husband appreciates her natural beauty. "She looks best to me when she takes seven minutes to get together and we go out low-key," says Gavin.

THE SWEET ESCAPE

Being a new mom didn't slow down Stefani at all. While she recorded songs for her new album, baby Kingston hung out in the studio. An easygoing, friendly baby, he quickly became acquainted with the team of musicians, producers, sound mixers, and other assistants who surrounded his famous mom.

Stefani collaborated with talented musicians and producers from her first solo album, such as Nellee Hooper, Dave Stewart, and Tony Kanal. The first single on the album, "Wind It Up," was produced by the Neptunes.

In December 2006, Stefani released her second solo album, *The Sweet Escape*. On her website, she noted how different her second album was from her first. "The dance sound is very 'now,'" says Stefani. "It's modern . . . not so retro."

On "Wind It Up," Stefani fulfilled her dream of incorporating *The Sound of Music* into her own music. She begins the hip-hop track by yodeling part of "The Lonely Goatherd," a song from the musical. In the song's video, Stefani wears a nun's habit, modeling herself after the character Maria in the movie. The Harajuku Girls make a reappearance—this time with freshly dyed blonde hair—helping Stefani act out various scenes from the musical.

Gwen performs "Wind It Up" with her Harajuku dancers at the 2006 American Music Awards in Los Angeles, California.

However, the hybrid song didn't go over as well as 2004's "Rich Girl," her first attempt at adding a beat to a song from a musical (in that case, *Fiddler on the Roof*). While "Wind It Up" peaked at number six on the *Billboard* charts, it didn't fare well on the radio. A writer from *USA Today* called "Wind It Up" the worst song of the year. The critic continued, "Stefani may have thought she was in a league of her own and could get away with anything, but she forgot one paramount rule: There's no yodeling in pop music."

Fortunately, other singles from *The Sweet Escape* were more popular than the first. The album's bouncy title track topped the *Billboard* Pop 100 chart in early 2007. Though other female artists such as Fergie and

Nelly Furtado had produced major hits during Stefani's time off, Stefani showed that she could still reign as the queen of pop.

She also continually surprises her fans with her multidimensional talent. The star happily revealed her first fragrance in March 2007. Stefani collaborated with Coty Prestige to create the perfume, called *L* (for "love"). *L* is a medley of sweet and exotic scents, including lily of the valley, rose, violet leaves, water hyacinth, sweet pea, and orange blossoms.

She enjoyed her venture into perfume-making tremendously. She felt that designing a fragrance was a prestigious sign that her company was a success. Stefani planned to create more fragrances too. The woman who had once worked the perfume counter at The Broadway department store had come a very long way.

Stefani and the Harajuku Girls hit the road together in April 2007 for *The Sweet Escape* World Tour. The tour swept the United States first, with a sold-out opening night in Las Vegas. It continued on to international destinations such as Mexico, Australia, and Ireland. In August of 2007, *The Sweet Escape* World Tour appeared in both Tokyo and Osaka, Japan—marking Stefani's first solo performances in the country that originated the Harajuku style.

"FILLED UP WITH EVERYTHING"

Stefani wants to continue to be a fashion designer. She may even create a men's clothing line one day, she says.

But for the time being, designing has to take a backseat to her roles as a mom and a musician. In the future, she plans to give her full attention to designing.

Stefani has other aspirations too. She'd like to perform in a musical. The singer would also like to learn to play the guitar. If she did, she wouldn't have to rely on someone to collaborate with. She figures that she could write all her own music if she had that skill.

Stefani remains modest about her success. "I'm definitely fooling people every single day," she says. "I'm like everybody else." Stefani also handles the pressures of fame well. But she has to be careful not to overcommit herself. She has learned to set boundaries to avoid being overwhelmed by life in the public eye. And in spite of all her goals for the future, she is able to appreciate her remarkable achievement thus far.

"I feel pretty filled up with everything," she says. "I feel like maybe I can take a breath and go, 'OK, I've done all these things; now I can just enjoy the moment.'"

However, relaxing doesn't seem to come easy to Stefani. The gifted musician is also a champion multitasker. She thrives when she has many creative projects in the works. Bold, glamorous, funky, and sweet, the busy pop star is someone to watch—and listen to. In her art, music, and personal life, Stefani is constantly evolving and full of surprises.

MAJOR AWARDS AND HONORS

GRAMMY AWARDS AND NOMINATIONS
BEST FEMALE POP VOCAL PERFORMANCE
2005, "What You Waiting For?" Nominated
2006, "Hollaback Girl" Nominated

RECORD OF THE YEAR
2006, "Hollaback Girl" Nominated

BEST POP VOCAL ALBUM
2006, *Love.Angel.Music.Baby.* Nominated

BEST RAP/SUNG COLLABORATION
2002, "Let Me Blow Ya Mind" Won
2006, "Rich Girl" Nominated

ALBUM OF THE YEAR
2006, *Love.Angel.Music.Baby.* Nominated

MTV VIDEO MUSIC AWARDS
BEST MALE VIDEO AWARD
2001, Moby/Gwen Stefani, "South Side"

BEST FEMALE VIDEO AWARD
2001, Eve/Gwen Stefani, "Let Me Blow Ya Mind"

BEST GROUP VIDEO AWARD
1997, No Doubt, "Don't Speak"
2002, No Doubt, "Hey Baby"
2004, No Doubt, "It's My Life"

BEST POP VIDEO AWARD
2002, No Doubt, "Hey Baby"
2004, No Doubt, "It's My Life"

BEST CHOREOGRAPHY AWARD
2005, Gwen Stefani, "Hollaback Girl"

BEST ART DIRECTION AWARD
2005, Gwen Stefani, "What You Waiting For"

TIMELINE

1969 Gwen Renee Stefani is born in Fullerton, California, on October 3.

1986 Gwen joins her brother's band, No Doubt, and shares vocals with John Spence.

1987 No Doubt gives first public performance, in Long Beach, California. Tony Kanal joins the band. He and Gwen begin dating. Gwen graduates from high school.
John Spence commits suicide. Gwen takes over lead vocals.

1991 No Doubt signs a recording contract with Interscope Records.

1992 *No Doubt*, the band's first album, is released. No Doubt goes on its first national tour.

1994 Eric Stefani quits the band to pursue a career as an animator. Gwen and longtime boyfriend, guitar player Tony Kanal, break up.

1995 No Doubt independently releases *The Beacon Street Collection*. *Tragic Kingdom* is released. Gwen meets Gavin Rossdale, leader of the alternative rock band Bush. They begin dating.

2000 *Return of Saturn* is released.

2001 No Doubt's fifth album, *Rock Steady*, is released. Gwen performs on Eve's "Let Me Blow Ya Mind."

2002 Gwen marries Gavin Rossdale on September 14.

2003 Gwen releases first L.A.M.B. designs: handbags. No Doubt releases *The Singles 1992–2003*.

2004 Gwen releases her first solo album, *Love.Angel.Music.Baby*. She also appears in her first movie role, as actress Jean Harlow in *The Aviator*.

2005 In September, Gwen presents her first runway show at New York Fashion Week. Gwen's solo tour hits the road. Gwen announces her pregnancy in the final concert of the tour.

2006 Gwen gives birth to son Kingston on May 26. She releases her second solo album, *The Sweet Escape*, in December.

2007 *The Sweet Escape* World Tour begins in April, taking Gwen and the Harajuku Girls all over the world.

Source Notes

7   Ariel Levy, "The Coronation of Gwen Stefani," *Blender*, December 2004, http://www.blender.com/guide/articles.aspx?id=1329 (August 23, 2006).

8   Jenny Eliscu, "Gwen Cuts Loose," *Rolling Stone*, January 27, 2005, 36–40.

8   Ibid.

9   Ibid.

14 Denise Henry, "Gwen Stefani," *Scholastic Action*, October 3, 2005, 4–5.

14 Jennifer Kasle Furmaniak, "It's Good to be Gwen Stefani," *Cosmopolitan*, June 2004, 60–64.

15 Michele Sponagle, "She's Just a Girl," *Flare*, June 2005, 60–64.

17 Susan Swimmer, "Gwen Stefani: I'm a Very Different Gril [sic] Than I Used to Be," *Marie Claire*, June 2005, 74–80.

17 Merle Ginsberg, "A Fashionable Life: Gwen Stefani," *Harper's Bazaar*, September 2005, 313–316.

19 Jenny Eliscu, "Gwen Cuts Loose."

22 "Timeline," No Doubt Official Website, http://www.nodoubt.com/band/ (May 4, 2007).

23 Ariel Levy, "The Coronation of Gwen Stefani."

23 Lorraine Ali, "It's My Life," *Newsweek*, September 6, 2004, 47–48.

24 Susan Swimmer, "Gwen Stefani: I'm a Very Different Gril Than I Used to Be."

24 *No Doubt Web* (unofficial No Doubt website), http://www.nodoubtweb.com/history.htm (May 4, 2007).

24 Ibid.

26 Ariel Levy, "The Coronation of Gwen Stefani."

26 Lorraine Ali, "It's My Life."

26 Jenny Eliscu, "Gwen Cuts Loose."

28 Susan Swimmer, "Gwen Stefani: I'm a Very Different Gril Than I Used to Be."

28 Jennifer Kasle Furmaniak, "It's Good to be Gwen Stefani."

28 "Solo Stefani: A Lion in Lamb's Clothing," *USA Today*,
    November 23, 2004, 01d.
29 Lorraine Ali, "It's My Life."
31 No Doubt Official Website, http://www.nodoubt.com/ (May
    4, 2007).
32 Chris Heath, "Snap! Crackle! Pop!," *Rolling Stone*, May 1,
    1997, 36.
32 Ibid.
34 Ibid.
34 Lorraine Ali, "It's My Life."
36 Ariel Levy, "The Coronation of Gwen Stefani."
36 Ibid.
36 Jonathan Bernstein, "Absolutely No Doubt," *YM*, April
    1997, http://www.nodoubt.com/press/articles/
    36YMMag.asp (March 13, 2007).
36 Jonathan Bernstein, "Gwen Stefani," *The Face*, July 1997,
    n.p.
36 Ariel Levy, "The Coronation of Gwen Stefani."
41 "Timeline," No Doubt official website,
    http://www.nodoubt.com/band/ (May 4, 2007).
42 "Without a Doubt," *People*, January 28, 2002, 79.
43 Phoebe Eaton, "Gwen's Secrets," *Harper's Bazaar*, March
    2005, 322–327.
44 "Timeline," No Doubt official website,
    http://www.nodoubt.com/band/ (May 4, 2007).
45 Isaac Guzman, "No Doubt about Stefani: Gwen's Eclectic
    Choices Keep Her at the Top," *Daily News* (New York),
    December 19, 2001, n.p.
47 Ibid.
48 Ibid.
48 Ibid.
49 Alanna Donovan, Author telephone interview with a Gwen
    Stefani fan, Alanna Donovan, February 16, 2006.
49 Isaac Guzman, "No Doubt about Stefani: Gwen's Eclectic
    Choices Keep Her at the Top."
49 "Without a Doubt."
50 Ibid.
50 Ibid.
50 Brantley Bardin, "No Doubt About It," *InStyle*, February
    2003, 264.

50 Ariel Levy, "The Coronation of Gwen Stefani."

51 Jennifer Kasle Furmaniak, "It's Good to be Gwen Stefani."

53 Isaac Guzman, "No Doubt about Stefani: Gwen's Eclectic Choices Keep Her at the Top."

53 Lorraine Ali, "It's My Life."

53 Jennifer Kasle Furmaniak, "It's Good to be Gwen Stefani."

53 Ibid.

54 Ibid.

54 Selene Milano and Suzanne Zuckerman, "The Stylemakers: Gwen Stefani," *InStyle*, November 2004, n.p.

54 Susan Swimmer, "Gwen Stefani: I'm a Very Different Gril Than I Used to Be."

55 Pam Huwig, "Gwen Stefani," *Lesbian News*, May 2005, 20–21.

55 Ibid.

58 Ariel Levy, "The Coronation of Gwen Stefani."

58 Jenny Eliscu, "Gwen Cuts Loose."

58 Ibid.

58 "Solo Stefani: A Lion in Lamb's Clothing."

59 Ariel Levy, "The Coronation of Gwen Stefani."

59 Michael Endelman, "Gwen Stefani," *Entertainment Weekly*, December 30, 2005, 58–59.

60 Jancee Dunn, "Gwen Stefani," *Rolling Stone*, December 30, 2004, 86.

60 Ariel Levy, "The Coronation of Gwen Stefani."

60 Chuck Taylor, "Luxurious," *Billboard*, November 11, 2005, 59.

60 Chuck Taylor, "Crash," *Billboard*, February 11, 2006, 83.

62 Alanna Donovan, Author telephone interview with a Gwen Stefani fan, Alanna Donovan, February 16, 2006.

62 Edna Gundersen, "A Solo Stefani is Fun, No Doubt About It," *USA Today*, November 23, 2004, 04d.

62 Michael Endelman, "Gwen Stefani," *Entertainment Weekly*, December 30, 2005, 58–59.

62 Michael, Melissa Heide, and Asal Tataei, "Letters," *Flare*, September 2005, 42.

63 Susan Swimmer, "Gwen Stefani: I'm a Very Different Gril Than I Used to Be."

63 Jenny Eliscu, "Gwen Cuts Loose."

64 MiHi Ahn, "Gwenhana: Gwen Stefani Neuters Japanese

Street Fashion to Create Spring's Must-have Accessory: Giggling Geisha!," *Salon.com*, http://dir.salon.com/story/ent/feature/2005/04/09/geisha/index.html (October 4, 2006).

64 Pam Huwig, "Gwen Stefani."

65 Ibid.

65 Ibid.

65 Phoebe Eaton, "Gwen's Secrets."

65 "Beauty Amazing Face," *Teen People*, June/July 2004, n.p.

66 Jennifer Kasle Furmaniak, "It's Good to be Gwen Stefani."

66 "Aboard 'Aviator' Time Machine," *USA Today*, December 3, 2004, 02e.

67 Hannah Betts, "Suicide-blonde Stefani Has a Little L.A.M.B.," *The Times* (London), January 5, 2006, 10.

67 Craig Rosen, "Gwen Stefani," *Hollywood Reporter—International Edition*, October 25, 2005, 20.

67 Chuck Arnold, "Gwen Stefani," *People*, December 6, 2004, 47.

67 Hannah Betts, "Suicide-blonde Stefani Has a Little L.A.M.B."

67 Selene Milano and Suzanne Zuckerman, "The Stylemakers: Gwen Stefani," *InStyle*, November 2004, n.p.

69 Pam Huwig, "Gwen Stefani."

71 "Fashion: Patrol," *Teen People*, March 2005, 85.

71 Susan Swimmer, "Gwen Stefani: I'm a Very Different Gril Than I Used to Be."

71 "Solo Stefani: A Lion in Lamb's Clothing."

72 Jennifer Kasle Furmaniak, "It's Good to be Gwen Stefani."

72 Michele Sponagle, "She's Just a Girl."

72 Merle Ginsberg, "Gwen at Work."

73 Michele Sponagle, "She's Just a Girl."

73 Pam Huwig, "Gwen Stefani."

74 Hannah Betts, "Suicide-blonde Stefani Has a Little L.A.M.B."

99 Stephanie Thompson, "Who Are You Wearing? Why, it's a Gwen," *Advertising Age*, September 12, 2005, 12.

75 Alison Maxwell, "Gwen Stefani's L.A.M.B. Roars onto NYC Catwalk," *USA Today*, September 19, 2005, 04d.

75 "Rock 'n' Runway," *People*, October 3, 2005, 105–106.

76 Ibid.

76 Elio Iannacci, "Fashion Moment," *Flare*, December 2005, 44.

77   "Stars Design," *People*, April 12, 2006, 95.
77   Phoebe Eaton, "Gwen's Secrets."
78   Ibid.
79   "All-star CD to Help Hurricane Victims," *USA Today*, October 17, 2005, 01d.
79   Jenny Eliscu, "Gwen Cuts Loose."
81   Geoff Boucher, "Looking Forward to Her Love Angel Music Baby," *Toronto Star*, December 29, 2005, A29.
82   Michael Endelman, "Gwen Stefani."
82   Geoff Boucher, "Looking Forward to Her Love Angel Music Baby."
83   Donna Freydkin, "Designer/mom Hat Fits Gwen Stefani to a T," *USA Today*, September 15, 2006, 14d.
83   Geoff Boucher, "Looking Forward to Her Love Angel Music Baby."
86   "Gwen Stefani & Gavin Rossdale," *People*, June 12, 2006, 66–67.
87   Hannah Betts, "Suicide-blonde Stefani Has a Little L.A.M.B."
87   Michele Sponagle, "She's Just a Girl."
88   Clarissa Cruz, Melissa Goldberg, Elizabeth Lamont, Samantha McIntyre, and Kara Murphy, "Gwen's Brand New Bag," *People*, September 4, 2006, 153.
88   Merle Ginsberg, "Gwen at Work."
89   Michele Sponagle, "She's Just a Girl."
90   Jennifer Kasle Furmaniak, "It's Good to be Gwen Stefani."
91   Susan Swimmer, "Gwen Stefani: I'm a Very Different Gril Than I Used to Be."
91   Michele Sponagle, "She's Just a Girl."
91   Merle Ginsberg, "A Fashionable Life: Gwen Stefani."
92   Ibid.
92   Phoebe Eaton, "Gwen's Secrets."
93   Merle Ginsberg, "Gwen at Work."
93   Merle Ginsberg, "A Fashionable Life: Gwen Stefani."
93   Jennifer Kasle Furmaniak, "It's Good to be Gwen Stefani."
93   Phoebe Eaton, "Gwen's Secrets."
93   Merle Ginsberg, "Gwen at Work."
94   Alison Maxwell, "Gwen Stefani's L.A.M.B. Roars onto NYC Catwalk."

94 Gwen Stefani Official Website, http://www.gwenstefani.com.
95 "The Highest of the Low Notes," *USA Today*, December 26, 2006, 06d.
97 Michele Sponagle, "She's Just a Girl."
97 "Solo Stefani: A Lion in Lamb's Clothing."

SELECTED BIBLIOGRAPHY

"Aboard 'Aviator' Time Machine." *USA Today*, December 3, 2004.

Adkins, Greg, et al. "Gavin's New Secret Daughter." *People*, November 1, 2004.

"A Baby Boy for Gwen, the Red Lipstick Mother." *Mail on Sunday*, May 28, 2006.

Ahn, MiHi. "Gwenihana: Gwen Stefani Neuters Japanese Street Fashion to Create Spring's Must-have Accessory: Giggling Geisha!" *Salon.com*. http://dir.salon.com/story/ent/feature/2005/04/09/geisha/index.html (October 4, 2006).

Ali, Lorraine. "It's My Life." *Newsweek*, September 6, 2004.

"All-star CD to Help Hurricane Victims." *USA Today*, October 17, 2005.

Arnold, Chuck. "Gwen Stefani." *People*, December 6, 2004.

Author telephone interview with a Gwen Stefani fan, Alanna Donovan, February 16, 2006.

Bardin, Brantley. "No Doubt About It." *InStyle*, February 2003.

Bernstein, Jonathan. "Gwen Stefani." *The Face*, July 1997.

Betts, Hannah. "Suicide-blonde Stefani Has a Little L.A.M.B." *The Times* (London), January 5, 2006.

Boucher, Geoff. "Looking Forward to Her Love Angel Music Baby." *Toronto Star*, December 29, 2005.

Clebatoris, Jac. "Is Gavin a Dad? No Doubt." *Newsweek*, November 1, 2004.

Clebatoris, Jac. "Ms. Stefani Regrets. In a Major Snarky Way." *Newsweek*, September 5, 2005.

Cruz, Clarissa, Melissa Goldberg, Elizabeth Lamont, Samantha McIntyre, and Kara Murphy. "Gwen's Brand New Bag." *People*, September 4, 2006.

Dubin, Danielle, Eleni Gage, Liza Hamm, Samantha McIntyre, and Kara Murphy. "Racks of L.A.M.B." *People*, July 25, 2005.

Dubin, Danielle, Eleni Gage, Samantha McIntyre, Kara Murphy, and Jenny Sundel. "Gwen, Again." *People*, August 29, 2005.

Dunn, Jancee. "Gwen Stefani." *Rolling Stone*, December 30, 2004.

Eaton, Phoebe. "Gwen's Secrets." *Harper's Bazaar*, March 2005.

Elliott, John. "Gwen Stefani and Gavin Rossdale." *Sunday Times* (London), September 24, 2006.

Eliscu, Jenny. "Gwen Cuts Loose." *Rolling Stone*, January 27, 2005.

Endelman, Michael. "Gwen Stefani." *Entertainment Weekly*, December 30, 2005.

"Fashion: Patrol." *Teen People*, March 2005.

"Fever Chart." *Entertainment Weekly*, October 14, 2005.

Freydkin, Donna. "Designer/mom Hat Fits Gwen Stefani to a T." *USA Today*, September 15, 2006.

Freydkin, Donna. "Gwen Stefani: Hair Apparent." *USA Today*, October 31, 2005.

"Frock 'n' Roll." *People*, February 16, 2004.

Furmaniak, Jennifer Kasle. "It's Good to be Gwen Stefani." *Cosmopolitan*, June 2004.

Gage, Eleni, et al. "Rock of Ages." *People*, December 20, 2004.

Ginsberg, Merle. "A Fashionable Life: Gwen Stefani." *Harper's Bazaar*, September 2005.

Ginsberg, Merle. "Gwen at Work." *Vanity Fair*, Fall 2005 Special Issue.

Gundersen, Edna. "A Solo Stefani is Fun, No Doubt About It." *USA Today*, November 23, 2004.

Guzman, Isaac. "No Doubt about Stefani: Gwen's Eclectic Choices Keep Her at the Top." *Daily News* (New York), December 19, 2001.

"Gwen Stefani & Gavin Rossdale." *People*, June 12, 2006.

Gwen Stefani Official Website, http://www.gwenstefani.com.

Heath, Chris. "Snap! Crackle! Pop! *Rolling Stone*, May 1, 1997.

Henry, Denise. "Gwen Stefani." *Scholastic Action*, October 3, 2005.

Huwig, Pam. "Gwen Stefani." *Lesbian News*, May 2005.

Iannacci, Elio. "Fashion Moment." *Flare*, December 2005.

Jenkins, Elizabeth. "No Doubt About It." *InStyle*, Spring 2006 InStyle Weddings.

Levy, Ariel. "The Coronation of Gwen Stefani." *Blender*, December 2004. http://www.blender.com/guide/articles.aspx?id=1329 (August 23, 2006).

"Life Swap," *Vanity Fair*, September 2006 Supplement.

Maxwell, Alison. "Gwen Stefani's L.A.M.B. Roars onto NYC Catwalk." *USA Today*, September 19, 2005.

Milano, Selene, and Suzanne Zuckerman. "The Stylemakers: Gwen Stefani." *InStyle*, November 2004.

"My Favorite Decade." *People*, September 20, 2004.

No Doubt Official Website, http://www.nodoubt.com/.

No Doubt Web (an unofficial No Doubt website), http://www.nodoubtweb.com/history.htm.

Rayner, Ben. "Move Over Madge." *Toronto Star*, December 10, 2005.

"Rock 'n' Runway." *People*, October 3, 2005.

Rosen, Craig. "Gwen Stefani." *Hollywood Reporter—International Edition*, October 25, 2005.

"Solo Stefani: A Lion in Lamb's Clothing." *USA Today*, November 23, 2004.

Souter, Ericka, et al. "Bye-bye Baby Weight!" *People*, September 18, 2006.

Sponagle, Michele. "She's Just a Girl." *Flare*, June 2005.

Stack, Tim. "L.A.M.B. Shop." *Entertainment Weekly*, October 7, 2005.

Swimmer, Susan. "Gwen Stefani: I'm a Very Different Gril Than I Used to Be." *Marie Claire*, June 2005.

Taylor, Chuck. "Crash." *Billboard*, February 11, 2006.

Taylor, Chuck. "Luxurious." *Billboard*, November 5, 2005.

Thompson, Stephanie. "Who Are You Wearing? Why, it's a Gwen." *Advertising Age*, September 12, 2005.

Tucker, Reed. "Gwen Stefani." *Fortune*, October 17, 2005.

"Without a Doubt." *People*, January 28, 2002.

FURTHER READING
AND WEBSITES

BOOKS

Blankstein, Amy H. *The Story of Gwen Stefani*. New York: Omnibus, 2005.

Tracy, Kathleen. *Gwen Stefani*. Hockesin, DE: Mitchell Lane Publishers, 2006.

WEBSITES

No Doubt (Official Website).
    http://www.nodoubt.com
    Watch videos, listen to songs, and read interviews and articles at the official No Doubt site.

Gwen Stefani (Official Website).
    http://www.gwenstefani.com
    Get the latest news and tour dates at Gwen's official site, which also hosts videos, songs, and a photo gallery.

INDEX

OTHER TITLES FROM TWENTY-FIRST CENTURY BOOKS AND BIOGRAPHY®:

Ariel Sharon
Arnold Schwarzenegger
Benito Mussolini
Benjamin Franklin
Bill Gates
Billy Graham
Carl Sagan
Che Guevara
Chief Crazy Horse
Colin Powell
Coretta Scott King
Daring Pirate Women
Edgar Allan Poe
Eleanor Roosevelt
Fidel Castro
Frank Gehry
George Lucas
George W. Bush
Gloria Estefan
Gwen Stefani
Hillary Rodham Clinton
Jack Kerouac
Jacques Cousteau
Jane Austen
J.K. Rowling
Joseph Stalin
Latin Sensations
Legends of Dracula
Legends of Santa Claus
Malcolm X

Mao Zedong
Mark Twain
Martha Stewart
Maya Angelou
Napoleon Bonaparte
Nelson Mandela
Osama bin Laden
Pope Benedict XVI
Pope John Paul II
Queen Cleopatra
Queen Elizabeth I
Queen Latifah
Rosie O'Donnell
Russell Simmons
Saddam Hussein
Shakira
Stephen Hawking
The Beatles
Thurgood Marshall
Tiger Woods
Tony Blair
Vera Wang
V.I. Lenin
Vladimir Putin
Wilma Rudolph
Winston Churchill
Women in Space
Women of the Wild West
Yasser Arafat

ABOUT THE AUTHOR

Katherine Krohn is the author of many award-winning juvenile biographies, fiction, and books on contemporary issues. She lives in the Pacific Northwest.

PHOTO ACKNOWLEDGMENTS

The images in this book are used with the permission of: © Stephane Cardinale/People Avenue/CORBIS, p. 2; © John Shearer/WireImage.com, p. 6; © Richard Cummins/SuperStock, p. 10; © CinemaPhoto/CORBIS, p. 15; © Ron Wolfson/WireImage.com, p. 18; © UPPA/ZUMA Press, p. 20; © Barry King/WireImage.com, p. 25; © Bud Fraker/John Kobal Foundation/Getty Images, p. 27; © Kelly A. Swift/Retna Ltd., p. 30; © Jim Smeal/WireImage.com, p. 33; © Joe Giron/CORBIS, p. 37; © Tim Mosenfelder/Getty Images, p. 38; © Kathy Hutchins/ZUMA Press, p. 40; © Neal Preston/CORBIS, p. 46; © Interscope Geffen A&M Records/ZUMA Press, p. 51; © Donald Miralle/Getty Images, p. 55; © Frank Micelotta/Getty Images, p. 56; © Kevin Winter/Getty Images, p. 59; AP Photo/Mark J. Terrill, p. 61; © Yuriko Nakao/Reuters/CORBIS, p. 63; © Vince Bucci/Getty Images, pp. 66, 80; AP Photo/Jennifer Graylock, p. 68; © Fernando Salas/ZUMA Press, p. 73; AP Photo/Stuart Ramson, p. 76; © Lucy Nicholson/Reuters/CORBIS, p. 84; © Karl Larsen/ZUMA Press, p. 86; © Todd Plitt/Getty Images, p. 89; © Sharjo/Express UK/ZUMA Press, p. 90; © Ethan Miller/Getty Images, p. 95.

Front cover: © Bryan Bedder/Getty Images.
Back cover: © Barry King/WireImage.com.

WEBSITES